During all of life's transitions, grace,
courage and success is yours to claim.
Be strong and eagle-like and know
you are never alone. God is The
Eagle Maker, catch the wind of
His Spirit and soar!

12-15-12

Reg Kll

The Eagle Maker

God's Grace During Job Transition

———◆———

Regina K. Leigh

CROSSBOOKS
PUBLISHING

CrossBooks™
A Division of LifeWay
1663 Liberty Drive
Bloomington, IN 47403
www.crossbooks.com
Phone: 1-866-879-0502

First published by CrossBooks 11/12/2012
ISBN: 978-1-4627-2218-1 (sc)
ISBN: 978-1-4627-2219-8 (e)
ISBN: 978-1-4627-2220-4 (hc)
Library of Congress Control Number: 2012920518

Printed in the United States of America

This book is printed on acid-free paper.

Any people depicted in stock imagery provided by Thinkstock are models,
and such images are being used for illustrative purposes only.

Certain stock imagery © Thinkstock.

Because of the dynamic nature of the Internet, any web addresses or links contained in
this book may have changed since publication and may no longer be valid. The views
expressed in this work are solely those of the author and do not necessarily reflect the views
of the publisher, and the publisher hereby disclaims any responsibility for them.

Unless otherwise indicated, Scripture quotations used in this book are from the Holy Bible, New International Version.

Grateful acknowledgement is made to the following for permission to reprint previously published material:

Bob Hatcher, *The American Bald Eagle: Recovery from Extinction* (Vanderbilt University, 2011)

Elisabeth Kübler-Ross & David Kessler, "The Five Stages of Grief" (Grief.com, 2000–2012)

Nell W. Mahoney, *You Can Soar Like an Eagle* (Nashville: Dimensions For Living, 2004)

Peter Laue, "Molting Eagles" (Cambridgedove.com, 2009)

Rhay Torres, *A Painful Season of Our Lives: Molting* (Friend of The Bridegroom, 2010)

American Bald Eagle Information, Bald Eagle—Nesting & Young (baldeagleinfo.com, 2012)

Rebecca L. Grambo, *Eagles* (Voyageur Press, Inc., 1999)

Merriam-Webster Online (www.Merriam-Webster.com) copyright © 2012 by Merriam-Webster, Incorporated.

Christian Spiritual Life Journal, Weavings, 1991

Al Siebert PhD, *The Survivor Personality*, (Berkley: Perigee Books, 1996)

This book is dedicated to my husband, Tom, whom I adore. He believed in me even when I didn't. He possesses a great balance between staying grounded and dreaming big—a gift that continually provides for our family and makes our life rich in possibilities. Even during the extreme rawness and vulnerability throughout the loss of our franchise, he made so much possible. I love how we laugh together, and I admire his quick wit. I especially thank him for reminding me to have faith and be faithful as I put the finishing touches to these pages.

Contents

Foreword

I believe that everything happens to us for a reason and a purpose. The loss of your job unexpectedly is devastating. For many, your occupation is who you are. It cuts to the fiber of your ego. You question, "What did I do wrong? What could I have done differently?" Losing a job is very similar to losing a close relative or a family through a divorce. You experience a whole range of emotions, denial, anger, bargaining, depression, and acceptance. The stages of grief do not necessarily happen in that order and are often experienced again and again.

I knew a person whose job was eliminated. He was not successful in finding a new career after several months. I was saddened to learn that he committed suicide. Knowing how to deal with your emotions after losing a job is vital.

When a life crisis happens, I believe it is God's way of getting our attention. He is calling for us to be closer to Him. He also wants to teach us something. First, seek God with all your heart, soul, and mind. Then ask Him, "Lord what do you want me to learn from this experience?" Study the Bible, fellowship with others, and do not be too proud to ask for help.

The good news is that God created you and loves you so much. We are His children, and good fathers want the best for their children. God wants the best for you. I hope you find comfort, strength, and encouragement from the words of this book. God will use this for good, if you let him.

Thanks to Regina for all her hard work and for her faithfulness with the Job Transition Group, which is founded on 2 Corinthians 1:3–4.

> Praise be to the God and Father of our Lord Jesus
> Christ, the Father of compassion and the God of all
> comfort, who comforts us in all our troubles, so that we

can comfort those in any trouble with the comfort we ourselves receive from God.

William Wright

Founder of the Williamsburg Job Transition Group in 2003. His vision was to create a ministry that provided encouragement, coaching, and comfort to those who lost their jobs or were seeking to change jobs or careers.

Acknowledgments

I want to first acknowledge God's presence and love in my life. He is the source of the words, lessons, and truths in this book.

Friendships are true treasures from God, and my friendship with Suzy Mulford is a real blessing. Her dedication as my editor was unfailing. Thank you, Suzy, for keeping me on point and grammatically correct. Your contributions in preparing this manuscript are invaluable. I couldn't have had a better partner in prose. More importantly though, I thank God and His divine intervention on the day you were "at a food show in Williamsburg and ran into my (your) dear friend, Regina …"

Thanks to Stan Mulford, for being my resident theologian.

I thank and give praise to William Wright, the founder of the Williamsburg Job Transition Group. He created a much needed ministry for our community. His vision for sharing God's love and divine grace during the trials and tribulations of job loss, changing careers, and finding employment provided me the sanctuary I needed to heal, which now makes all this possible.

I wish to acknowledge my friends Jay Faggart and Eunice Forehand. Jay is a support member of the Job Transition Group and community advocate for individuals faced with addictions. Jay was there when I first came to the Job Transition Group and was instrumental in my transformation through continued words of encouragement and assured faith. During my journey, each time I asked, "Who knew?" Jay pointed heavenward, saying, "He did!" Eunice introduced me to the notion of exploring eagles as a means to make my own way in leading the Job Transition Group. If I were to ask her, "Who knew I'd be writing a book?" she might silently mimic Jay's pointing toward heaven, but then she would probably shrug her shoulders, wide-eyed, and have a warm smile on her face.

John D. Rockefeller is quoted as saying, "A friendship founded on business is better than a business founded on friendship". This is truly the case with my relationships with Gil and Carolyn Petrina. I am ever grateful for, and blessed by, the mutual respect and support we give and receive from each other. It is exciting to see how we are soaring together as partners and as friends.

Many thanks to all the Job Transition Group members past and present. Your insistent encouragement, asking, "When is the book coming out?" brought me here today. I am honored each week that you allow me a platform to give back.

I wish to mention my late, beloved dog, Banner. We shared nearly fourteen years together. She was there for most of the highs and low mentioned in this book. I thank God for giving her to me. Her soulful eyes could touch anyone's heart. She freely gave hugs—they were the best. She truly was a source of comfort, lying by my side, during many of the tears shed during my "molting season."

Introduction

Whether referencing the Bible, math, or science, the number three holds great significance, to the point that we say that all things complete are imprinted with the number three. In math and science, the three dimensions of length, breadth, and height are necessary to form a solid and also stand for that which is real, substantial, and complete.

In the Bible, there's the Trinity (although you won't find the word "Trinity" in the Bible). There were three gifts to baby Jesus. Three days before the Ascension, three days in the belly of a fish. Peter denied Christ three times. The angels sing, "Holy, holy, holy." I could go on and on. And then there are God's attributes of omniscience, omnipresence, and omnipotence. My dear friend Suzy says, "I know that when God says something three times, you had better listen up."

My story of the power of three started with something I got that wasn't meant for me. One day, I received an e-mail that was addressed to someone else. It was an invitation to the Christian Business Network of Hampton Roads' upcoming luncheon. I had not heard of CBN and knew I had not signed up to be on their mailing list, so I looked to see who had sent it to me. When I looked at the "To" box, much to my surprise, there was a different person's e-mail address. No, it wasn't someone else's name, whereby if I right clicked on it, my e-mail address would be revealed. It literally was someone else's e-mail address. It read,

theirfirstname(dot)theirbusinessname@cox.net.

I was already intrigued by the invitation to go to the luncheon, but when I saw that, I figured it was God telling me I had to be there! So I quickly hit the link to register and eagerly waited for the date of the luncheon to arrive.

At the luncheon, the guest speaker opened with the old joke most of us know …

> A guy was stuck on an island in a flood, and as the river rose, a rescue team threw him a rope. But he refused to grab it, saying, "God will save me." The river rose higher and the rescue team sent a boat. Again he refused, saying, "God will save me." When the river waters rose to his chest, the man climbed a flagpole. A helicopter came, but he still refused their help, saying, "God will save me." But the river rose and the man was swept away. Curious and miffed, the drowned man, standing before God, asked, "Why didn't you save me?" God simply replied, "I sent you a rope, a boat, and a helicopter. What more do you want?"

That joke became the basis for the speaker's message of God's provision when we are in need. If God wants us to know something, to really get our attention, or to remind us to have faith, God will do so again, and again, and again. Throughout his message, the speaker kept referencing God's "knock on our door." He mentioned two other things that came to have tremendous significance a little later on that day. The first was, "There is a reason you are all here today," and the other was, "Don't underestimate the power of three."

After the speaker was finished, I was so energized that I quickly filled out my new member form and joined the group. I also decided to fill out the form to take out a small ad in their member directory, ShepherdsGuide.com. They came around and collected the forms and proceeded to draw for the door prizes as we finished our lunches.

There were three bags: one for business cards of all guests (you dropped one in as you came in the door), one for new members, and one for directory members. They started with the drawing from the business card bag, and—lo and behold—guess whose name was drawn. You guessed it. I won a CD.

Next, they drew from the new members bag, and guess whose name was drawn. I know. I couldn't believe it either! In amazement, I quickly

xiv

spoke up and thanked them, but said that since I had already won, they should draw another name. They did.

Happy that I was already a winner, I just sat there while they drew for the third door prize. To be honest, I have to admit I really wanted the third door prize. It was a collectible "Canyon Guardian" eagle from Ted Blaylock's *Winged Protectors* collection. Not that I wanted to be selfish or anything, but naturally I was drawn to it. In my mind, however, I was thinking, *What are the chances that my name would actually be drawn three times?* But guess what. I know. I couldn't believe it either! What are the odds that someone's name would be drawn not just once, not twice, but three times?

Tapped into the guest speaker's message now, I graciously accepted. Moved to tears, I got up and asked them if I could say something. I told the group that I did not want to appear greedy for taking the eagle but explained that I was writing a book called *The Eagle Maker* and I knew, like the guest speaker had said, there was the reason God had called me to this luncheon.

In that moment, I heard someone across the room shout out, "The power of three!" Another said, "It's meant for you to have." After the luncheon finished, people were coming up to me in tears and saying they really wanted the eagle, but when they heard my story, they knew God wanted me to have it.

After that luncheon, I knew I had to quickly move forward on publishing this book. It is based on a ten-week series that I developed as the weekly devotionals for the Job Transition Group that I lead in Williamsburg, Virginia. This group was God's instrument in helping me overcome the emotional and financial devastation associated with losing a retail store and the dream that I had worked so hard to build.

This group's help and refuge came full circle when the members asked me to be its leader in the fall of 2010, when the incumbent facilitator was going through his own job transition and was moving out of the area. I accepted, but never thought I'd be here today, so passionate about wanting to help those who are experiencing similar emotions and circumstances.

Being an advocate for the unemployed, and facilitating the Job Transition Group, is what I consider my passion and my ministry. I want to help people understand the grieving process as it pertains to job loss, help them regain their self-esteem, and learn to soar again.

While many people understand the grieving process in many of life's crises, many don't recognize that individuals experiencing job loss and unemployment will grieve in the same way. Additionally, there is a loss of dignity and self-worth, along with feelings of being lost, displaced, or abandoned.

Having my name drawn three times is proof to me that there such a thing as divine intervention. *The Eagle Maker—God's Grace during Job Transition,* demonstrates my human capacity to fly again. Winning that eagle was an affirmation that I am doing the right thing.

With the drawing of my name three times, I knew God was saying, "Have faith." And like Suzy says, I'd better listen.

Preflight Check

Before you begin your journey with the eagle, you must first recognize the eagle as a source of inspiration and courage. It instinctively knows it can fly! It must be confident. It cannot be doubtful. It must be strong.

How do you feel right now? Do you feel vulnerable? Weak? Tired? Do you have more negative emotions or more positive?

Loss of a job, long bouts of unemployment, and a transition in positions/careers are life crises. So much of who we are is tied to how we make a living: how we pay our bills, provide for our family, even how we engage in fun and entertainment. Depending on the circumstances surrounding the change, especially change from employment to unemployment, feelings connected to loss and crisis arise.

Before beginning the first chapter, take a moment to look at each of the following charts and grade your current state of fragility and empowerment. Chart 1 assesses feelings of helplessness and hopelessness, all emotions clearly connected to job crisis. Chart 2 illustrates words used to describe eagle-like characteristics and eagle-minded people.

On a scale of 1 to 10, rank how you feel in this moment. In each chart, put a check mark in each row associated with each word. On the lower end of the scale, 1 pertains to a low sense of that feeling, and 10 relates to having a high sense of that feeling.

Don't be afraid to have a good, honest look at yourself. Remember feelings are not facts and do not make you a failure. The fact is you are God's creation, God's child. Just because you are feeling low and inadequate doesn't mean you are.

Chart 1

At first, your scores may be at the high end of the scale. That is perfectly normal. Over time, as you begin to acquire more eagle-like qualities, your scores should shift from the right to the left, dropping from the higher numbers to the lower numbers.

Date:	Somewhat							Overwhelming		
	1	2	3	4	5	6	7	8	9	10
Raw										
Exposed										
Picked Apart										
Deflective										
Negative										
Depressed										
Defenseless										
Lack of Desire										

These eight emotions represent words that are drawn from the eagle analogies throughout this book. They are, by no means, the only emotions tied to the highs and lows of job transition and unemployment. For now, you may feel more connected to emotions such as fear, doubt/uncertainty, frustration, isolation, anger, and shame. There are many, many more. You are not alone. Each week I speak with hundreds of people. Although each person's story is unique, the feelings and emotions are similar.

With so many emotions, it is no wonder that the sense of feeling overwhelmed can clip our wings. You will want to take a look at this chart throughout your journey and gauge your progress. You should see the balance tip as your negative emotions decrease and your positive attitudes increase.

<u>Chart 2</u>

Just as the emotions listed in Chart 1 share a common thread, so too, do the attributes listed in this chart. During times of strife, people often feel challenged to see their own value. Compromised emotions can quickly diminish our capabilities. Today, your scores may be at the lower end of this scale. That is OK. It is important to be honest. Do not be afraid to admit what you are having difficulties with right now.

Date:	Less Strong								More Strong	
	1	2	3	4	5	6	7	8	9	10
Self-Aware										
Determined										
Disciplined										
Confident										
Faithful										
Resilient										
Respected										
Compassionate										

As you begin to watch, listen, and assimilate, your scores will shift from left to right. This book will help you to right your frailties. When they have reached the higher numbers, you are taking flight!

Chapter 1: In the End

Blessed is the man who perseveres under trial, because when he has stood the test, he will receive the crown of life that God has promised to those who love him.

—James 1:12

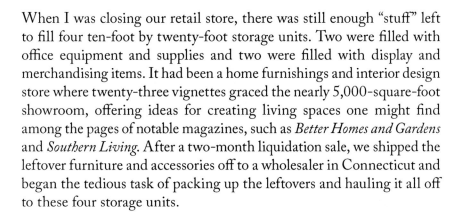

When I was closing our retail store, there was still enough "stuff" left to fill four ten-foot by twenty-foot storage units. Two were filled with office equipment and supplies and two were filled with display and merchandising items. It had been a home furnishings and interior design store where twenty-three vignettes graced the nearly 5,000-square-foot showroom, offering ideas for creating living spaces one might find among the pages of notable magazines, such as *Better Homes and Gardens* and *Southern Living*. After a two-month liquidation sale, we shipped the leftover furniture and accessories off to a wholesaler in Connecticut and began the tedious task of packing up the leftovers and hauling it all off to these four storage units.

There were more than 4,000 fabric swatches, dozens of rug samples, in-store signs and their stands—just tons of things that when put in their respective places made sense. These were the items that helped run daily operations. They kept things organized. They aided our employees and designers. They helped customers make choices. To me, each was associated with a story. Some items told stories I'd rather forget.

It was overwhelming to see it all piled up, everything on top of the other. Every time I had to open any one of those units, two battles raged. The first was associated with my Type A personality, which wanted things neat and organized; the second was tied to the visual representation of the chaos whirling around me. A dream that took four years to build, from a culmination of fifteen years of experience, was ending by only one year of circumstances beyond my control.

Which do you feel carries more weight? All the stuff piled in those lockers that took me seven sentences to describe or all the emotion piled into that one sentence of describing the loss of my dream?

Now before I go any further, I must clarify something. The dream of owning a successful storefront was only one-third of the equation. Another third of my dream belonged to the financial security I had built over the years that, according to plan, was supposed to only get bigger. The last third belonged to the culmination of fifteen years of experience, which in my mind's eye meant I was on track with my game plan for retirement.

Yes, all this stuff piled high in the storage units was indeed hard to let go of. But the truth was my attachment to these things was merely superficial. Years later, I now understand that the root of my attachment was the belief tied to losing it all. I felt robbed of my dignity, my self-worth, and my net worth! At first, it was about losing the store, then it was about losing the money, and in the end, I was left to confront the belief rooted in having to start all over again.

Is this your belief as well? Do you feel you have to start all over again too? Or perhaps you just don't know where to begin.

When were the constant reminders and the lessons all going to end? When were the head ache and heart ache going to end? This wasn't where I was supposed to be at this stage of my life.

Yes, I meant to separate the *ache* from each word. Had I said *headache* and *heartache*, the connection between what the mind thinks and what the heart feels may not have been so obvious. For me, while the head and heart function separately within our bodies, and one cannot function without the other, they are codependent in emotional behavior. In tandem, it is far too difficult to separate what we think from what we feel. This is how we humanly seek our answers. Our human selves seek answers from our environment and the influences of our circumstances rather than accessing the truth provided to us by God and the knowledge provided to us through His word. We tend to be so mentally or emotionally attached to the outcome we want that we are either oblivious or unresponsive to what God wants for us.

Since the knowledge to understand right from wrong, truth from falsehood, and good from evil are among God's gifts to us, then why is it so hard to hold fast to the right belief?

- *Right*, meaning that I know I am where God wants me to be from the *wrong* that I am not where I want to be.

- The *truth* in knowing that as a child of God I am perfect rather than the *falsehood* that I have failed or I am incompetent. Perfection in the biblical sense does not mean "without flaw." It means "complete." The Greek word is *telos*. It refers to the realization of purpose.

- Recognizing that there are so many more *good* things now, things that could not have existed before, because of the veil of *evil* that shrouded things during the turmoil of closing the store.

Do find yourself teetering back and forth on these points? If you nodded yes, you are not alone. Indeed, their juxtaposed nature leaves one struggling and feeling the impossibility of separating headache from heartache. If you have ever shouted, "I know! I know! Easier said than done!" or "Yeah, yeah, been there, done that!" then know that those cries belong to your human self. It doesn't matter if we hold them inside or truly shout them out. They are cries tied to our belief that this *is not* how things are supposed to be or we are not where we are supposed to be, no matter the context.

Spiritual enlightenment on a journey toward employment provides the tools to distinguish that which we want for ourselves and that which

God wants for us. Staying strong in God's love when chaos whirls around us provides the calm needed in order to let go of our attachment to personal desires and leads to trusting in God's plan.

> For I know the plans I have for you," declares the LORD,
> plans to prosper you and not to harm you, plans to give
> you hope and a future.

Jeremiah 29:10–12

I have always been a spiritual person with a strong faith in God and His word. Prior to this whole mess, you would have found me saying, "I believe" or "I have faith." It was this loss of nearly everything that had me teetering. As I tried to take it one breath at a time, one breath would hold my faith that there is a God, and as Scripture teaches, He will not forsake me, while the next breath would cry, "Why is this happening to me?" My broken heart could not be soothed. Though I was surrounded by friends and family, I felt so alone. No one lived and breathed that dream like I did. In my grief, it was so easy to believe that no one could truly empathize with me, which made my emotional state spiral downward that much faster.

I couldn't sleep at night because I could not turn off all the what-ifs in my head. Like the tail end of a movie reel that flaps noisily as the reel keeps spinning, all the decisions I could remember making over the store kept spinning in my head. And that annoying flapping sound accompanied each jump from thought to thought.

As the nighttime darkness filled my bedroom, I searched and prayed for how I could right things. Nothing made sense. How could it all be gone so quickly? I hadn't been given enough time to spread my wings. Not enough time to feel what it was like to truly soar in success and see my dream take flight. Without warning, my wings were clipped and I was grounded. Even worse, with no money left, I believed I would never fly again, even though people often fail multiple times before achieving great success. I felt more like an ugly duckling than a majestic eagle.

Week after week, I would sit in a daze at church, sometimes choking from trying so hard to hold back the tears. The reprieve I got from the pastor's message lasted only as long as I sat there. Often, the minute I got in my car and I was alone with my thoughts, the movie reel would start spinning again.

As I look back on what I have learned through this transition, I realize I should never have allowed this loss to define who I was. And neither should you. By allowing that to happen, one might say that I had my faith but I was not faithful. If only I had held up His promise in prayer.

> Restrain your voice from weeping and your eyes from tears, your work will be rewarded.
>
> Jeremiah 31:16

My hope is that you always hold on to the correct belief that a person's work, whatever it may be, now and in the future, is what God wants it to be.

Prayer

Dear Father, still our hearts and trembling hands. Help us find peace. We want to remain faithful, no matter how hard things become; show us the way. Through You, we are strong. Though we may now weep with tears of trouble, we know they will soon be tears of joy. Amen.

Chapter 2: In the Beginning

> For our light and momentary troubles are achieving for us an eternal glory that far outweighs them all. So we fix our eyes not on what is seen, but on what is unseen, since what is seen is temporary, but what is unseen is eternal.

2 Corinthians 4:17–18

———————◆•◆•◆———————

Previously, I mentioned that it took only one year of circumstances out of my control for a dream that took me four years to build, from a foundation of fifteen years of past experience, to end! To put that into perspective, I must take some time to put it into context. To understand the raw emotion of the low, you must understand the elated emotion during the high.

I grew up with a love for dance, which earned me my bachelor's degree. I paid my own way through college, working hard and taking out student loans. Because my right brain didn't pay the bills while I pursued my love for the arts, I worked in office jobs throughout college. There were jobs in bookkeeping and administrative work, which laid the foundation for my business acumen, which later included an MBA, several FINRA licenses, and several certifications.

Despite my corporate career, my wicked creative streak was always close behind. It must be the artist in me. My love for baking turned a hobby of making wedding cakes and confections into a weekend business for many years. My love for sewing is what got me hooked on interior design. As far back as I can remember, I made everything from window treatments to bed coverings and reupholstered furniture as well. Hallelujah! The store was finally going to allow me to have them custom made via vendors rather than make them myself!

So as you can see God, has truly blessed me with an awesome blend of right-brain/left-brain faculties and a strong entrepreneurial spirit. I've been called the dancing baker and the bean counter with moves, and was once told I dress "too normal" to be a dancer. Perhaps that was a foreshadowing of what was to come much later when I built my career as a financial and operations manager.

In 1992, I began working for an introducing broker-dealer. As the years progressed, ample opportunities came along to advance my career in corporate finance and the securities industry. In brief, I worked for them for ten years, earned three FINRA licenses, and traveled across the United States while integrating four branch offices. Because this all took place during the computer and Internet revolution, I was indeed in the first wave of computer commuting, and I experienced all the excitement of the dot-com surge and subsequent bust. I traveled a lot for both work and pleasure, and later you will hear me refer to this time as one of the heights of my career. This was indeed the time when I built my financial security and most of my retirement.

About a month prior to 9/11, I weathered the last of six acquisitions my company went through over ten years. Though I was one of the first employees to be let go, the rest of the employees soon followed after the new company took over. Then one month later, the events of 9/11 happened and I was up against finding a job in an economic sector that was whirling in instability. Despite all that, and it happening just seven months after the divorce from my first husband, I still felt young and brazen enough to know another opportunity would come along. Whew, the resiliency of a young heart!

Another opportunity indeed came along, and I landed back in the securities industry with a wealth-management firm. Although I managed to earn another FINRA license, I always felt I had taken five steps backward, having taken this job. I went from being a registered financial and operations principal (senior management) prior to 9/11 to being an administrative assistant to a portfolio manager in this new job. After a few years, it became clear that the advancement I sought to regain my prior status was more my need than theirs.

After many discussions with my husband (I remarried in 2003), I began to channel all of my corporate experience and entrepreneurial spirit into business ownership. Over the course of several years, I analyzed businesses and performed due diligence in order to determine which businesses suited my talents and desires. After narrowing the pool from hundreds to a dozen, and then down to the top three, I knew I had found the right one after watching a video which told the history and story of the four generations that built the franchise I was courting.

I had two criteria that had to be met. First, I wanted it to be a business that married my creative side with my business side. Second, I wanted to be able to say, "I am the proud owner of _____." At the end of this video, one of this company's founders said that very sentence almost verbatim. It was then I knew the choice would be this franchise with a 106-year history. A home furnishings store offering interior design services whereby I could pair my business acumen with my artistic flair.

We opened on Memorial Day 2007, with a wonderful ribbon-cutting ceremony that I hold dear in my heart. We exceeded budget through the end of the year and entered 2008 positioning ourselves for our first major floor reset and making the necessary adjustments as we learned, as every new business does.

But as our one-year anniversary approached, and we were just getting our foothold in the marketplace, some things seemed "off" with our franchisor. We were being told the modifications they were implementing were a result of the changes in the furniture and textile industries as a whole. We persevered, but by September, we learned these "modifications" were a guise and the franchisor had filed bankruptcy.

If losing our investment in the franchise wasn't bad enough, we lost the money sent to the franchisor for custom orders placed prior to their filing bankruptcy. We had to return customer deposits for custom orders that were never shipped and had to build new vendor relationships, which narrowed margins for filling the orders for customers who hung in there with us.

My husband and I began calling it the perfect storm. The salt to the wound was the downturn in the economy one month later, which was October 2008.

Not only had sales dropped off because consumers were in a wait-and-see mode with spending their discretionary income, but there was also the stigma now associated with the franchisor. Every day we had to guard against losing customer loyalty, as well as our footing in the marketplace. We were committed to pressing on and communicated that to our customers, but that also was met with a wait-and-see attitude. All of this impacted sales.

In the midst of this operational turmoil was the intellectual turmoil. I was finding it hard to keep up. Every business lesson ever learned, practical or textbook, was tapped. It almost seems silly to say it was an emotional roller coaster.

The first wave of intense emotional strife was centered in how this would impact our employees' livelihoods. For those serving in support and operations, their hours would be cut back. For the designers, the decrease in sales affected their commissions. I didn't want anyone to leave, nor did I want to put my employees in the unemployment lines. I was so wrought with anxiety over it that I spoke up during one of my church's Sunday services and asked for everyone's prayers that my employees would be safe and provided for.

The second emotional discord, and certainly the longest lasting, was the grief associated with putting my family through all this. I had always been an equal provider in my household, and here I was taking all their security away. My husband's job was secure (he continued to work outside the store), but that did not prevent us from being thrust into living from paycheck to paycheck and quickly becoming behind both at the store and at home.

As I tried to make sense of all that was going on, I began knocking on every door from the Small Business Administration to the governor's office, seeking help and possibly some of the stimulus money they said was out there. It was all in vain. Addressing that adventure could be a book in and of itself.

We hung on for one more year, but as sales continued to slow, and the stress of the economy and survival loomed, we made the tough decision to close.

We didn't walk away unscathed. My husband and I reached deep into our own pockets to close the store with our heads held as high as possible. In the end, we lost everything except our house and our two cars. All the financial security we had built to get to the point of owning a store that was to take us on to retirement was gone.

In the chapters to follow, you will learn how broken, how disjointed, and what an emotional wreck I was while trying to emerge from closing this store. Like any life crisis, it was both a revolutionary and evolutionary process. No matter whether you consider your transition to be that of a job, a career change, or another type of life crisis, such change is a life alteration.

I would not say that I felt suicidal, but the sense of giving up frequently washed over me—even though I didn't quite know what giving up meant. In hindsight, I liken it to an eaglet that has been pushed from its nest into a vast unknown. No matter how vigorously I flapped my wings, I could not catch the wind. Like a scared eaglet, gripped in fear, I saw the approaching ground and felt impending doom. I kept trying to fly. I wanted to fly! So I kept going through the motions, not knowing what would happen next.

Anyone going through a life crisis will say that what makes the journey so hard is not knowing what will happen next. For those experiencing unemployment and going through the arduous task of looking for a job, what brings the first wave of fear is not knowing how long it will take. Getting to a point where I could fly again took a lot of perseverance and remaining mindful that I had to have faith in that which is unseen.

Though it seemed like forever, in God's time I made it through. Like an eaglet caught by its Father, I was caught in His embrace.

Prayer

Heavenly and gracious Father, we have known great joy, and great sorrow. You have been by our sides through it all, and we are forever grateful. As our journey continues, we know You will provide comfort and peace. Amen.

Chapter 3: The Eagle Soars

Though you have made me see troubles, many and bitter, you will restore my life again; from the depths of the earth, you will again bring me up. You will increase my honor and comfort me once more.

Psalm 71:20–21

———————◆•◆•———————

During my days as a financial operations principal, I felt like an eagle—although I did not possess the understanding I do today of this bird's grandeur and complexity. I would have been referring only to the bird's ability to soar high above the mountaintops, skimming the billows of the clouds and dancing in the rays of the sun. Now in my quest to tell the story of how I made it from the highs of my career to writing this book, I have learned so much more. God brought this bird to me so that I may see His plan for me and truly understand the words of Isaiah.

Those who hope in the LORD will renew their strength.
They will soar on wings like eagles.

Isaiah 40:31

The eagle is a bird having found favor with God and there are numerous scriptural references to its strength and majesty. The eagle's tenacity to take flight during a storm is why we value eagles as symbols of courage and inspiration.

Those who come to know the wonderful characteristics of eagles seek to be eagle-like. Whether instinctual or deliberate, what makes people fly like eagles in the face of adversity is their faith and steadfast belief that God's everlasting arms will carry them through. How they react to the challenges before them is what makes them soar.

Everyone encounters a life crisis at some point. In fact, it is safe to say that most people will experience several over the course of their lifetime. Many call these storms. Some storms may be nothing more than gusts of winds with rain lasting a few hours to perhaps a couple of days. Other storms are more life changing, such as my perfect storm that spanned several years. One year of picking up the pieces from a defunct franchise, one year of dealing with the aftermath of closing the doors, and many, many months of trying to find my way again.

Job transition and job loss certainly are storms. You may feel this job transition is the worst one yet. Think about that for a moment … How did you react when you first learned you had lost your job? How are you reacting now? Do you feel your emotional state has improved or gotten worse? As time has gone on, have your emotional barriers to employment increased?

Even if your scores in chart 1 are at the higher end of the scale right now, have faith. As we continue to explore the eagle, you will learn how to draw upon the inner resources that come from your ability to use that which God provides to rise above and soar like an eagle.

Given their size and wingspan, an eagle's flight may be awkward at first. But once it catches the wind, pure grandeur begins. They have learned to use their God-given talents with God's natural resources to glide and circle in a way we see as effortless. We too are unique, equipped with characteristics, features, and attributes designed by God, that will help us soar effortlessly. We just need to learn to channel our efforts and our faith to accomplish that which seems impossible in the chaos whirling around us.

In Psalm 139, verses 7 through 10, the psalmist sings that God is always with us, holding us, and lifting us, yes, even in times such as these ...

Where can I go from Your Spirit?

Or where can I flee from your presence?

If I ascend into heaven, you are there;

If I make my bed in hell, behold, you are there.

If I take the wings of the morning,

and dwell in the uttermost parts of the sea,

even there your hand shall lead me,

and your right hand shall hold me.

How are you reacting in this storm of unemployment? In this storm of transition?

This is truly a time when the old adage rings true: you may not be able to change your circumstances, but you can change how you react to them. Your circumstances may be out of control, but you are not. The first step to overcoming your transition is to understand that it is a grieving process. We will explore the stages of grieving in a later chapter, but for now, you must recognize this as fact and accept its consequence. You will need to allow yourself the time to get through it, just as you would in any type of loss.

Loss of a job is devastating. Not being able to find employment is even worse. Our dignity and self-esteem are shaken. Loss of dignity means a loss of worthiness and feeling less respected. When we lose our self-esteem, we lose our poise, our positioning, and our ability to make a favorable impression on others. In the book, *The Five Stages of Grief,* we are told that it is essential for each of us to experience grieving in order to live beyond the circumstances that define our loss. I know, for those in the Job Transition Group, that grief between one job and the next is very real. The unfortunate truth is each of us may be surrounded by family and friends who don't recognize the grief we are experiencing.

At the very moment one loses one's job, the sense of unworthiness sets in. The longer time goes on with attempting to become gainfully employed, the lower our self-esteem becomes. The two only get worse when those around us start to judge us for moodiness and inability to secure a job in what they consider to be "a reasonable amount of time."

There are many books written about the grieving process. I encourage you to find one to study in depth, perhaps even find a support group specifically for grieving. The grieving process *is* real as it pertains to job loss, and it is something you must understand in order to soar again.

The stages of grieving are denial, anger, bargaining, depression, and acceptance. There is no set order in which these emotions are experienced. And just as in grieving any type of loss, the emotions will be codependent on each other and you will experience ebbs and flows. Just when you feel you have conquered one, something may happen and you may experience a setback.

In the stage of *denial*, things seem overwhelming and little makes sense. You will wake wondering how you will make it through the day, and you will probably go to bed feeling drained. You are in a state of shock and are not in tune with your emotions. How long you remain in denial is dependent on your state of fragility and the support you surround yourself with. Even eagles rely on each other for support, as you will later learn. The sooner you begin to accept the reality of the situation, the sooner you will begin to heal.

Most experts in the study of grieving will agree that *anger* is the hardest stage to deal with. It is frustrating that people seem so willing to accept one's anger over the loss of a loved one or divorce but want to rob us of it during job transition. I have heard people say, "Suck it up," or "Being angry isn't going to solve anything." During my own experience, I got even angrier when that happened. Why was I not allowed to feel angry about what I was experiencing? Why shouldn't I feel confused about where I was, or should I say where I was not, at that point in my life?

It is okay to feel anger. Experts say the more you allow yourself to feel the anger, the more quickly you will move on. Trying to deny it or suppress it will only hold back the healing. Wallowing in it too long isn't healthy either. It will hold you back.

The state of *bargaining* is one of compromise and guilt. Your thoughts and actions are framed in the context of "What if I …" or "If I just …" It is filled with self-imposed guilt, and when you may be setting yourself up for future failure, because it is unlikely we will uphold our end of the bargain. When you find yourself starting a thought or a sentence with "What about …" or " What if …," stop for a moment and reflect on what I am saying here. If you find you are bargaining or compromising, you may be setting yourself up for unhappiness later. Oftentimes, we believe taking something is better than nothing. Such compromises can sometimes lead to further resentment, stress over no longer having the time to look for the job you really want, and deeper feelings of diminished self-worth—especially if the pay is not what we want or need. Be sure to discuss all options with the family members that will be affected, and be confident the decision you make will yield the result <u>everyone</u> wants. During these discussions, be clear about what will and will not make everyone happy, including on- and off-job responsibilities and short falls in monetary contributions. Determine not only your expectations of short- and long-term planning, but the expectations of your family as well.

Depression is a normal and an appropriate response to job transition. Digging deeper, however, there are emotions of diminishment, separation, sorrow, shame, desolation, and ignorance—all emotions deeply rooted in depression. It is natural to want to withdraw and become isolated, but you will have to find a balance between wanting to be by yourself and engaging in people activities. Let others lift you up. Draw from their energy. Rely on others to keep you in check. If you find you cannot strike a balance, I encourage you to seek professional help.

Acceptance is the recognition of what is no longer, and what the new reality holds. In job loss, it is accepting that you will no longer be doing the same thing, you will no longer be working with the same people, and in some cases, you may not earn the same amount of money. When you accept such losses and do not allow them to define who you are, or you worthiness, then you are on the road to recovery.

As I mentioned earlier, there will be people around you who do not understand the grieving process as it pertains to job transition. The best thing you can do for yourself is to find a support group that does not deny the grieving process and will help you make sense of it. These are the people I call eagle-like people. Watch, listen, and assimilate their thought and speaking patterns. Their thoughts will be positive. How they communicate will invariably be more positive. This is such a critical component to getting through our crisis that we will explore this throughout the book. The single most important influence in our lives is the people we hang around with. Be present with them. Let their compassion and encouragement begin to renew your faith. They will help you face your crisis with courage and hope.

Prayer

Dear Lord, in Your Word, in Isaiah: 40:31 it says,

> But those who hope in the Lord will renew their strength. They will soar on wings like eagles; they will run and not grow weary, they will walk and not be faint.

Walk with us, oh, Lord, so that we find courage to go forth this week and be an eagle. Grant us in Your grace and learn to channel our efforts for Your good.

Be ever present and remind us to use the positive examples of friends, family members, coworkers, and neighbors, those we see as eagle-like, to guide us. For we know that when we use these God-given sources, we can *soar like an eagle!* Amen.

Chapter 4: An Eagle Falls

> Finally, brothers and sisters, whatever is true, whatever
> is noble, whatever is right, whatever is pure, whatever is
> lovely, whatever is admirable—if anything is excellent
> or praiseworthy—think about such things.
>
> Philippians 4:8

———————◆•◆•◆———————

There are nearly sixty species of eagles around the world, and in my research, I have found two characteristics they share that resonate with me. The first is the role the father eagle plays in teaching his young to fly and the second is their molting season. While there are so many wonderful and awe-inspiring qualities to explore, these two encapsulate the essence of Philippians 4:8 and signify the pain that I endured when losing my store, and my beginning toward healing.

In the first chapter, we concluded that spiritual enlightenment during job transition helps us distinguish that which we want for ourselves and that which Gods has planned for us. In the third chapter, we began to learn how the eagle uses natural resources provided by God to take flight. You were encouraged to seek out other eagle-minded people and use Scripture to begin to channel our efforts and find hope.

The first steps to putting all those together are to learn how to assimilate eagle-like tendencies. You will need three things:

o   You must learn what makes an eagle majestic and spiritual, literally and figuratively. The coming chapters explore both.

o   You will need to surround yourself with people who demonstrate eagle-mindedness and symbolic behavior. Later, I will share who I hung out with and how their influence came to be the source for my transformation.

o   Finally, you will need the support of God's Word. Like an eagle, its striking power is tremendous and will be discussed in greater detail later.

Look! An eagle will soar and swoop down, spreading its wings ..."

Jeremiah 49:22

So what makes the eagle so majestic, so courageous, and so spiritual?

Eagles are known for using thermals (updrafts) to stay aloft and soar without flapping their wings. This is what makes their gliding across the skies seem so effortless. Each wing has twelve hundred feathers with wing slots at the end between the large and primary feathers. These slots maximize their ability to increase lift and assist in maneuvering—all God-designed features that make them unique. This lift and maneuverability, along with their high speeds, plays an important role in both the highs and lows of the eagle's flying.

Most everyone knows that eagles fly very fast. Typically, their speed is between forty and sixty miles per hour. When diving, they can reach speeds up to one hundred miles per hour. This ability to fly and dive fast not only helps in hunting, but it is the foundation that builds its family.

Once paired, eagles are mates for life. It all begins when a male eagle becomes interested in a female eagle, and he begins to fly near her, waiting for a sign of her interest. If she is not interested, she will fly away. If she is interested, she will begin putting him through a series of tests that will determine his worthiness.

The female will throw a twig toward the ground for the male suitor to dive and retrieve before it hits the ground. If he is successful, she will perform this ritual multiple times, each time getting closer to the ground before releasing the stick. If the male eagle misses just once, he will be deemed unsuitable. But if he is successful at his quest, they will "marry."

The male's speed, agility, and perseverance are key during this ritual. It is how the female eagle knows he will protect his family. As the father, he will participate in teaching his young eaglets to fly by circling above the nest as the mother nudges her baby out of the nest for the first time. He will keep his eyes on his offspring as it falls toward the ground and will dive to catch it if the eaglet does not catch the wind. This continues until the eaglet has learned and begins soaring on its own.

This is not unlike God's love and His everlasting arms waiting to catch us when we fall. Yes, in one sense I am referring to the falling on hard times and needing to be picked back up. But on a much, much deeper level, I am referring to letting go.

In the early stages of my transition from losing the store, the time between making the decision to close the store and finding my Job Transition Group, I had my faith but I was not faithful. Often, I felt too tired to go to church and thought if I just lay in bed and prayed, it would be enough (bargaining). I intentionally isolated myself from people who could lift me up because their optimism seemed too daunting (depression). It was always in the front of my mind that I was once told I would be a terrible poker player because my face gives too much away. Therefore, my social interaction was stifled. Who wanted to be around an old sourpuss like me anyway, right?

When I finally found the Job Transition Group, things began to change. They made me feel safe. On the days I could smile, I felt their empathy, and on the days I could share a minor triumph, they helped celebrate. Most importantly though, they helped me realize misplaced emotions (anger) that kept me at the periphery of His embrace.

I have learned that it is not until we are broken, or have fallen, that God can work with us. We have to be able to admit that we need Him. He will not come to us until he is invited. And so, He vigilantly waited, keeping His eye on me. When I finally got to the point that I realized I had to let go, and I stepped over the ledge into a freefall of pure faith, that is when He quickly swooped in and took me into His everlasting arms so we could soar together.

As you go through your grieving process and you feel like you are falling, let yourself fall. You just have to believe that when the hardships of being without a job, looking for a job, and starting all over again overwhelm you, you mustn't lose sight of the truth: God can soar faster than any eagle to catch His own child—you!

Prayer

Dear Lord, How many times do I rely on myself instead of letting You catch me? I want to know Your safety and Your comfort. Help me recognize the times I need to let go in order to receive Your greater good. I want to feel the everlasting arms. I do not want to be on the periphery of Your embrace, and I am extending my hand to You. Amen.

Chapter 5: An Eagle's Eye View

Do you have eyes but fail to see, and ears but fail to hear? And don't you remember …?

Mark 8:18

———————◆◆◆———————

How many times have you heard someone say, "By the grace of God?" Have you not been filled with sorrow before but overcome it? Have you not been ill and recovered? Have you ever felt you were at your breaking point but made it to the other side? Was that not done by the *grace of God*?

Staying focused on God's glory and grace is very hard in a world plagued by pessimism. When naiveté, emotion, and fear took over shortly after learning the franchisor was filing bankruptcy, I wanted to believe in God's grace, but with all that was going on, I could only live in the moment (denial).

Would you say that God has provided a miracle for you at some time in your life? Then why is it so difficult for you to think He will not perform one during your job transition?

It wasn't until much later while hanging out with my Job Transition Group that I began to recognize how distinct yet similar "seeing beyond the moment" and "seeing the big picture" are. Without this understanding, I could not have transitioned into something better (acceptance).

A quick Google search will yield millions of returns on the fact that an eagle's sight is about three to four times sharper than ours, and it can spot its prey from about a mile away. An example I was once given, to put that into perspective, is an eagle's ability to determine if a coin is facing heads up or heads down from that distance. Its sight has two centers of focus, much like the zooming in and out when looking through binoculars. It is this dual ability of focus and clarity that is behind the expression "eagle eyes." Someone who has the ability to see the whole picture with clarity and focus is often described as having eagle eyes.

Although our human eyesight will never be as keen as an eagle's, God has given us our own unique abilities to see things with clarity and focus. We may lack zooming capabilities and our peripheral capabilities may not be as great as an eagle's, but we can think forward and backward at the same time. We look toward the future from learning from our past. Our intellect allows us to rationalize, surmise, and extrapolate the big picture.

Throughout life, you are presented with learning opportunities through both negative and positive circumstances. However, too often we are conditioned to dwell on what we learn from the negative experiences rather than the positive ones, especially during difficult times. When we are immersed in the challenges associated with joblessness, it may appear that there is nothing positive going on around us. Figuratively speaking, the speed at which we fall in a negative downward spiral is typically much faster than the speed we have when trying to rise back up. That is why it is so important to find clarity and focus as quickly as possible. Once you can do this, you will be able to see beyond your current circumstances and begin to see the possibilities of what is next.

Having eagle eyes not only means seeing the big picture; it also means seeing beyond the moment. In the gospel of Mark 8:18, we are reminded to look toward God and listen for what God is telling us. When the disciples crossed the Sea of Galilee with Jesus, they worried about not having any bread to eat, despite the fact they had just witnessed Jesus feeding thousands of people with five loaves of bread and two fish. Why do you think it was so difficult for them to see the bigger picture, to know that they too would be provided for? Had they not learned from very recent experience?

This passage reminds us to always use our eagle eyes to focus on the bigger picture and draw from our faith that with God, all things are possible.

In addition to having the unique dual-sight capability, eagles can look directly into the sun because they have two sets of eyelids: one is used for hunting and feeding and the other is a thin, translucent membrane that lowers and filters the sunrays. A newborn bald eagle's eyes are dark brown, fading first to a buff-brown and then gradually to a creamy color. However, once fully mature, its eyes turn yellow. Science says it's because they mature; I like to think it is because they are always looking into God's light and are transformed by its grace.

As often as possible during your transition, you should take a moment to truly connect to God's grace. Do this by facing the sun, closing your eyes, and lifting your face toward heaven. Take in a deep breath while remembering Mark 8:18. As you exhale, affirm, "Yes, Lord, I do have eyes to see and ears to hear." Repeat as many times as necessary until you feel His Holy Spirit wash over you. When you are ready, open your eyes to the glory of God.

Don't be afraid to repeat this exercise as often as necessary—several times throughout the day, if you have to. I will caution you, however, not to do it while driving or even while waiting for a red light to turn green. The car behind you may honk and startle you, as someone did to me one time.

> I lift up my eyes to the mountains—where does my help come from? My help comes from the Lord, the Maker of heaven and earth.
>
> Psalm 121:1–2

In the third chapter of Daniel, we are told our God is able. In order for us to be enabled, we must be able to see. In times of crisis, we must use our faith to see the big picture and stay focused, positive, and faithful. As Christians, we know if we allow the love and grace of Jesus Christ to flow through us, our lives can become witnesses to His power.

God grants us the power to overcome negativity. It is granted in our ability to focus on the right perspective. I once heard that coming in second place is being the first loser of the race. How sad is that? Staying rooted in that negative philosophy is closing your eyes to God's bigger picture. I have resolved to be more like Michele Kwan who, when asked by TV reporters during the 1998 Olympics, "How does it feel to lose the gold?" replied, "I didn't lose the gold. I won the silver!" What a shame the reporters did not see the bigger picture and dwelled only on the negative.

It is easy to soar like an eagle when we use our gifts from God purposefully and powerfully. There are many examples throughout history where people of power become great leaders because of their ability to see beyond the moment. When our nation was bankrupt and crippled in fear, Franklin D. Roosevelt said, "There is nothing to fear but fear itself." For some, those words initiated the recovery from the Great Depression. Winston Churchill, prime minister just six months, addressed the House of Commons by saying, "Let us brace ourselves and so bear ourselves, that if Great Britain and the Commonwealth last for a thousand years, men will say, 'This was their finest hour.'"

Both FDR and Churchill saw beyond the moment and used their eagle eyesight to inspire and motivate toward the bigger picture. With eagle eyes, they restored hope, glory, and grace.

Everything about the eagle's eyes points toward God. When you combine your eagle eyes with God's grace and glory, they just may glisten with a hint of gold!

Prayer

Dear Lord, bless us with Your strength and guide us to find the courage, like Daniel, to stand up to our accusers and fear nothing when thrown before lions. Keep us mindful to use the gifts You give us wisely. Guide us to stay focused on Your light. Reveal to us the big picture. Pull the cloak from our faces and show us all You have in store for us. Amen.

Chapter 6: He Nourishes Us

I will not leave you as orphans; I will come to you.

John 14:18

This will bring health to your body and nourishment to your bones.

Proverbs 3:8

———————◆•◆•◆———————

I mentioned earlier that during my transition with the store, I could not sleep. That threw off my whole eating schedule. My body never seemed to know when and when not to eat in relation to a normal breakfast, lunch, and dinner cycle. It seemed like I had an insatiable appetite.

Though I always seemed hungry, I typically ate only two meals a day. Finding the time to eat was a battle I put low on the list of priorities. Big mistake!

I would combine breakfast and lunch together around 10:30 to 11 a.m. and dinner much, much later. Sound familiar? Some people may not think that is bad. But it is. I knew this but persisted anyway. Furthermore, these meals weren't always healthy. At a time when I needed to be feeding myself a steady stream of healthy nourishment, I was refusing to help myself. Poor eating habits only add to lack of focus and inability to maintain clarity and stamina.

In your effort to find employment, you are going to have to do all you can to maintain these three attributes, including eating the right food so you can get you through the tedious application processes and writing résumés and cover letters that make you stand out among hundreds of applicants. Keeping your blood sugar levels stable and staying hydrated will help you face and overcome the highs and lows of prospects and rejections more easily.

Despite my poor judgment to make healthy eating more of a priority toward the tail end of keeping the store open, I was blessed in one very special way. My wonderful husband, Tom, would frequently bring me a home-cooked dinner that we would eat together at the store. Not only were these meals much more nutritionally balanced, but it was nice to have that time with him. He is a great cook and a good provider.

Likewise, both the mother and father eagles share in the responsibility to feed their newborns. They tirelessly fetch and bring back enough food. They are disciplined and determined to provide their young what they need to grow strong. As a result, the eaglets grow very fast. Golden eagles, for example, weigh only about three ounces at birth but will weigh forty times as much only forty-five days later. Providing for their children is not unlike God's provisions and care over us. In John 14, we are told that God will not leave us comfortless. He will come to us.

As eaglets, God provides all the nourishment we need in order to grow strong and take flight. Yes, literal food such as fruits, vegetables, meat, dairy, and grains—all the food that feed our bodies. The challenge is to make healthier choices and stay disciplined in order to stay strong.

I remember one day at the store, while talking with a friend, saying, "I'm so hungry, I can't think straight." She asked, "Then why don't you eat?" Replying that I didn't "have time" and tossing the notion out of my head surely didn't give me what God was telling me I needed. Looking back on it, God was trying to help me see what I needed, through my friend, but I was refusing to accept it.

How many times are you refusing to accept the seeds of knowledge, literally or figuratively? Especially when God has brought it straight to you like a parent brings food to its children.

Equally important are God's Word, His teachings, and the Holy Spirit, which are the food that feed our souls. It is the spiritual awareness, garnered through study, prayer, and reflection, that moves us toward heightened awareness of truth.

We have a wonderful guide and gift that is ours to embrace in our quest to live the truth, especially when challenging times try to separate us from the truth with shame, fear, guilt, vulnerability, and hopelessness. All of that wheedles its way at our psyche and veers us off our path.

Proverbs 3:7–8 confirms that God provides the nourishment we need.

> Do not be wise in your own eyes; fear the Lord and shun evil. This will bring health to your body and nourishment to your bones.

Without Scripture, our faith, and the acceptance of the Holy Spirit, we risk starvation of another kind: undernourished faith, which puts us at risk of being incapable of doing that which He has intended for us to do.

Prayer

Lord, guide me to Your wisdom. Help me recognize the seeds You plant around me and for me. Bring to me the right food to nourish my body. Feed me Your words and the breath of the Holy Spirit, so that I may become strong through You and in You. Amen.

Chapter 7: Striking Power

> Who redeems your life from the pit and crowns you
> with love and compassion, who satisfies your desires
> with good things so that your youth is renewed like the
> eagle's.
>
> Psalm 103:4:5

The state of vulnerability is difficult to understand. On one hand, we have the fragility that makes us susceptible to physical or emotional injury, criticism, and temptation. And on the other hand, we have the force that allows us to grow from the exposure or openness that is inherent in such a state. Vulnerability is often thought of as a weakness—a position or place we feel forced into. By definition, vulnerability is a state of being susceptible.

To the contrary, the Christian perspective allows for vulnerability to be thought of as the human capacity to be open, attracted to, touched, or moved by the draw of God's Holy Spirit. The expression of His love as experienced in one's own life or in the lives of others. The answer to the psalmist's question above lies in verse 6.

> The LORD works righteousness and justice for all the
> oppressed.

Did you know that the strike of the eagle's talon is so powerful that its force is twice that of a rifle's bullet? It is their keen eyesight and this fierce striking power that make them great hunters. Think of the Bible and how it too can have the same striking power. As an adjective, the dictionary puts "striking power" in the context of relating to an enemy, such as the capability of attacking an enemy or attacking a target effectively through space, as in "striking distance."

Initially that might seem negative; however, its synonyms are *remarkable* and *noteworthy,* as in the striking power of the Bible. Through its remarkable stories and noteworthy lessons, it is the best defense against your enemies of doubt, distress, anger, frailty, and hopelessness.

The Bible is filled with the never-ending message of God's grace, which is given freely for our continued regeneration and strengthening. It is filled with many people who faced affliction and hardship yet emerged on the other side in the arms of God. There are hundreds, right? Noah, Job, Moses, Jonah, David, Solomon, Ruth and Naomi, Mary, Peter and Paul … to name just a few. Each one of them forged on not knowing where his or her journey would lead. Each one made his or her own transition and became triumphant in his or her own right.

Like them, you may find yourself wondering why God is leading you through this experience. Are the highs and lows of job transition bringing an assortment of emotions that you find hard to manage? Perhaps hard to keep in control? In one minute, you may have hope in finding an opening that seems like the perfect match for your experience, and in the next, you may experience hopelessness when you didn't get the job you wanted. These emotional high and lows make it difficult for anyone to continue on.

> Do not be anxious about anything, but in every situation, by prayer and petition, with thanksgiving, present your requests to God. And the peace of God, which transcends all understanding, will guard your hearts and your minds in Christ Jesus."
>
> Philippians 4:6–7

In times of job transitions, doubts can overwhelm you. Often you will seem to be at the end of your rope and may get very distraught or angry. We have already discussed how you lose your dignity and self-esteem, but you may also begin to lose confidence in your abilities. "What did I do wrong?" "Why is this taking so long?" "What should I do next?"

In many ways, it makes you more aware of your own frailties. You panic, you question, and you lose sight of your priorities. More questions may be raised than answered.

o   Why aren't people returning my phone calls or e-mails?

o   Why do all my efforts seem useless?

o   Is God really hearing my cries?

To answer that last question, we need only to look at Jesus and His experience here on earth. Jesus' life was bound in complete trust, complete patience, and complete perseverance, even facing death as He fulfilled God's command and love for us. Although while on the cross, Jesus cried, "My God, My God, why have you forsaken me?" He knew His sacrifice carried the sins of the world and made complete His journey here on earth.

With the same conviction that an eagle hunts and provides for his family, we must remain steadfast in our journey to follow God's commands. As Christians, we become closer to God and receive the answers we seek by practicing complete trust, complete patience, and complete perseverance as Jesus did.

The Bible tells us you are not the only one to go through trials and tribulation and that you are not alone. Do you often cry out, "Is anyone out there who can help me?" In truth, you know you are not alone. It is only the dichotomy between truth and fragility that prompts us to cry out. So be honest: do you truly believe you are alone? The Bible assures us that we not, and Psalm 20 1:9 reminds us we will be both comforted and delivered.

May the LORD answer you when you are in distress;

may the name of the God of Jacob protect you.

May he send you help from the sanctuary

and grant you support from Zion.

May he remember all your sacrifices

and accept your burnt offerings.

Selah

May he give you the desire of your heart

and make all your plans succeed.

We will shout for joy when you are victorious

and will lift up our banners in the name of our God.

May the LORD grant all your requests.

Now I know that the LORD saves his anointed;

he answers him from his holy heaven

with the saving power of his right hand.

Some trust in chariots and some in horses,

but we trust in the name of the LORD our God.

They are brought to their knees and fall,

but we rise up and stand firm.

O LORD, save the king!

As you travel this unpredictable path called job transition, use the Bible as your armor. Experience its striking power. Hear the messages of those who have shared similar burdens. Through His word, the grace of the Holy Spirit will steady you. It will direct you and reveal His plan for you.

> For the Lord God does nothing without revealing his secret to his servants the prophets.

> Amos 3:7

Prayer

Heavenly Father, we long to be filled with Your Holy Spirit and the continued obedience to use the Bible to keep our enemies, fear, uncertainty, and doubt at bay. Arm us with the truth of John's word: "Do not let your hearts be troubled. Trust in God, trust also in me." Today we affirm that we trust in You, dear Lord. Amen.

Chapter 8: Eagle Lessons

> One thing I do: Forgetting what is behind and straining
> toward what is ahead, I press on toward the goal to win
> the prize for which God has called me heavenward in
> Christ Jesus.
>
> Philippians 3:13–14

———————◆•◆•◆———————

Job loss, long spells of unemployment, or changes in job responsibility can create helplessness. Associated financial challenges can cause
further strain in our family relationships. The hurt which comes from
feeling impaired or limited, criticized for not doing more to change
your circumstances, and the temptation to do things out of desperation
are the adverse reactions of feeling out of control. Often this feebleness
is misunderstood. You may not understand it, and those around you
may not either. You will wrestle with feeling like both the victim and
perpetrator. Your loved ones will struggle with their own emotions
of feeling victimized and finding the right balance between offering
support and prodding you along when you really need it. This is what
we addressed in chapter 3 when we garnered insights about the grieving
process. This lack of understanding can bring judgment, self-imposed or
perceived, based on what people around you are saying and doing.

If the circumstances under which you lost your job or had to change jobs
were bad, they can leave you in a state of paralysis. Invariably self-esteem

drops, and if you are like me, the movie reel I referred to earlier starts spinning.

It isn't anyone's intention to be weak and crippled by fear, but it can happen. In my case, I went from a person who used to be able to make decisions based on gut instinct to someone who couldn't make a decision until it seemed all facts had been uncovered. This inability to make things happen faster probably drove my husband crazy. In a nutshell, I wasn't who I used to be. And people's reassurances that what happened with the store was not my fault did little to make me feel less judged.

Such things can cause us to question not only what do we do now but where we belong. Be it job transition or any life crisis, remember you are a child of God. You belong to Him, and you belong where His Holy Spirit presides.

An affirmation is something declared to be true. Do you think an eagle awakens in the morning wondering, *Will I really be able to fly today?* No, he instinctively knows he can! Eagle-like people instinctively rise to the challenges before them.

Cultivating the right lessons in order to possess them instinctively and in the way God intends, especially during this time, sets us on the path to soaring. Here are just a few Scriptures that provide positive paths to change and help you replace doubt with absolute declaration.

o   Know you are an eagle with a strong spirit and that you can fly!

> Create in me a pure heart, O God, and renew a
> steadfast spirit within me.
>
> Psalm 51:10

> So do not fear, for I am with you; do not be
> dismayed, for I am your God. I will strengthen

you and help you; I will uphold you with my righteous right hand.

Isaiah 41:9–11

I can do all this through him who gives me strength.

Philippians 4:12–14

o   Remember your source of strength and armor.

> The LORD is my strength and my defense; he has become my salvation. He is my God, and I will praise him, my father's God, and I will exalt him.
>
> Exodus 15:1–3

> It is God who arms me with strength and keeps my way secure.
>
> 2 Samuel 22:32–34

o   Assimilate and practice. God wants you to be eagle like: strong, focused, mindful, good intentioned, and compassionate. Just as the eagle parents tirelessly feed their young, He wants to keep you nourished. Stay centered on Him and His Holy Spirit—read the Scriptures.

If you point these things out to the brothers and sisters, you will be a good minister of Christ Jesus, nourished on the truths of the faith and of the good teaching that you have followed.

1 Timothy 4:5–7

Praise be to the God and Father of our Lord Jesus Christ, the Father of compassion and the God of all comfort, who comforts us in all our troubles …

2 Corinthians 1:3–4

o   Remember eagles only hang out with other eagles. They will help you focus on your strengths and your value, not your limitations. They will help you spread your wings and fly.

Therefore encourage one another and build each other up, just as in fact you are doing.

1 Thessalonians 5:11

But encourage one another daily, as long as it is called "Today," so that none of you may be hardened by sin's deceitfulness.

Hebrews 3:13

Not giving up meeting together, as some are in the habit of doing, but encouraging one another—and all the more as you see the Day approaching.

Hebrews 10:25

o Eagles make great providers and they know their own worth. Understand that not all contributions have to be monetary. Your time and talents are just as valuable. Continually seek opportunities to contribute in your family and in your community.

> Which of you, if your son asks for bread, will give him a stone? Or if he asks for a fish, will give him a snake? If you, then, though you are evil, know how to give good gifts to your children, how much more will your Father in heaven give good gifts to those who ask him!

Matthew 7:9–11

o In their hour of need, eagles are compassionate to other eagles. Be kind to yourself and to others despite your frustrations and anger. Job transition is difficult enough without harboring animosity toward yourself and others.

> Be kind and compassionate to one another, forgiving each other, just as in Christ God forgave you.

Ephesians 4:32

> May God himself, the God of peace, sanctify you through and through. May your whole

spirit, soul, and body be kept blameless at the coming of our Lord Jesus Christ.

1 Thessalonians 5:22–24

For the eyes of the LORD range throughout the earth to strengthen those whose hearts are fully committed to him.

2 Chronicles 16:9

The Bible, no matter the condition of the book itself, will always produce wisdom. Scriptures are words to live by, and they are timeless. The knowledge, understanding, and experiences we have related to, in, and around the Bible are all tied to the truth of His Holy Spirit and will allow your spirit to soar.

Prayer

With Your help, dear Lord, from this day on, I will become more conscious of all that is creative and positive. I desire for my life to be more Christ centered, more efficient, and more effective, so that I may affirm, sow, and share a bountiful harvest. Amen.

Chapter 9: Flying with Eagles

> The eternal God is your dwelling place, and underneath
> are the everlasting arms.
>
> Deuteronomy 33:27

Whenever a bald eagle migrates south, it always returns to the same spot, and when it migrates north, it always returns to the same spot. These two places are its home. Habitat behaviors vary only slightly from species to species. Rarely do eagles move from nest to nest; instead, they add to their homes, making them bigger and bigger as the years roll by.

I make my home in Williamsburg, Virginia, home to the Historic Jamestown eagles' nest that rest in the treetops of Jamestown Island overlooking the James River. A pair of eagles has occupied that nest for about ten years now, and at least two eaglets have been born there. I have learned this nest is between eight and ten feet wide.

Eagles normally do not fly in formation, nor do they flock like many other birds. Yet it is not uncommon to see multiple eagles soaring among the treetops and mountain ridges during the same time. This is because they do have a strong sense of family and community, so multiple pairs may live in the same general area, especially mountainous regions. When I see them soaring together, I think of different instruments weaving in and out of a musical score. The notes and sounds of each individual instrument are wonderful, but together in a symphony they are wondrous.

As you begin thinking about the eagle-like people, groups, and networking opportunities you will now be interacting with, keep this analogy in mind. Each eagle-like person you encounter, and the knowledge he or she imparts, will be like a symphony. Notes will turn into scores. Scores will turn into movements. Movements will create a symphony. Their support will help you distinguish between the things you should do on your own and that which you should do with help, not unlike solos, duets, trios, and whole orchestrations. As the camaraderie and sense of family develop, you will feel stronger to stand alone with a rightful place in your community that should get bigger over time.

Often churches and small groups are referred to as home because people find sanctuary within their walls and among their people. Churches are a great place to find eagle-like people to hang out with. I mentioned earlier that I sought comfort and prayer from my church when my perfect storm arose. The first group I looked to for comfort was Stephen Ministries. It seemed like a good first step for sharing and seeking guidance. Through its one-on-one discretionary care and support, I quickly learned that truly "walking the walk" of my faith had waned. Remember … I had my faith, but I was not faithful.

The next group to learn the details of our store's troubles was my Disciple I class. It started right in the middle of all the insanity. It was six months after the franchisor filed bankruptcy but six months prior to the decision to close. This class is a one-year study of how to become a disciple through Bible study. I didn't take it because I felt worthy of being a disciple; I just wanted to learn Scripture more intimately. Through the lesson material, I did get to know the Bible better, but more importantly, I was able to be more focused in my prayers. Additionally, the members of the group were very supportive and offered a lot of advice about how to prioritize and deal with the customers.

In September of 2009, around the same time the store closed its doors for good, I was approached by a church member one Sunday after church service. He came to encourage me to attend a Job Transition Group that meets every Wednesdays at 7 a.m. He said it provides spiritual and emotional support for those experiencing a job loss or transition, and he thought I could benefit. I shamefully admit that at first I thought, *7 a.m. Yeah, right! I am tired enough as it is.* But something willed me to that upcoming week's meeting.

Thank God, they had coffee!

I should have been hesitant to go, seeing that I was a complete wreck—emotionally unstable, ready to cry at a moment's notice. In the first couple of weeks, as we went around the table to speak, I could not get anything out without welling up in tears. Sometimes I couldn't get it out at all. But God carried me there, week after week.

Between disciple class and the Job Transition Group, I was surrounded by a bunch of eagle-minded people. It took many, many months, but I eventually began to see, feel, and act faithful again. More like me. It was during one of the Job Transition Group's meetings that I finally let go and was *caught* by my Father.

It was on a day after the meeting when a member came up to me and said, "I can tell things aren't okay. It is written all over your face." Man, was I ever going to be able to have a poker face? We talked for a little bit about the constant reminders and my concern over money. It was five simple words that got me to let go. This eagle said, "You *are* better than this."

Driving home from that meeting, through the tears, I drew in a deep breath, gathering together all the unworthiness, and blew it out, affirming, "I *am* better than this." From that day forward, in His strength and guidance, I began to slowly get nourished and stronger. I watched, listened, and assimilated. These are the eagle lessons I learned from my community of like-minded eagles:

o **Do not deflect.** During difficult times, we feel judged. Try to determine if it is self-imposed. Often we are blind to see ourselves, our circumstances, and people for what they truly are.

o **Think positively.** Positive thinking can maximize our potential and opportunities and favorably impact our lives, experiences, and outcomes.

- o **Remain vigilant** in your faith, in your job search efforts, and in continuing to hang out with other eagles.

- o **Recognize the good.** See the old things passing away in your life, but stay focused on the new and good things being added.

- o **Be self-aware.** What are you conscious of? What do you understand? How are you responding?

Throughout life, you will have to demonstrate such assurance both in your walk of faith and in the secular world. It may not always be easy to marry the two. In fact, your moral compass may get frequently challenged during transition. Therefore, it will be especially important to understand the definitions of the key words in those lessons above.

- o Deflect: 1. Cause (something) to change direction by interposing something; turn aside from a straight course. 2. (of an object) Change direction after hitting something:

- o Positive: 1. The display of certainty, acceptance, or affirmation: a positive answer; positive criticism. 2. Measured or moving forward or in a direction.

- o Vigilant: 1. Keeping careful watch for possible danger or difficulties

- o Recognize: 1. Identify someone or something from having encountered him, her, or it before; know again: 2. Identify from knowledge of appearance or character:

- o Aware: 1. Having knowledge or cognizance: aware of the difference between the two versions; became aware of faint sound. 2. *Archaic* Vigilant; watchful.

Take a moment now to ask yourself, "Do I trust myself, my faith, and my relationships with those around me?"

When you can answer yes to each component of that question, you will know you are among the right sources of influence. Furthermore, you will have enough understanding of these five characteristics and how to integrate your faith in the secular world. You will know how to implement change with positive effect. You will be able to recognize danger and opportunity more readily because of your awareness. You will begin to demonstrate the type of confidence that can rise in adversity and face the storm, just as the eagle instinctively knows he can fly.

Prayer

By grace, God, You called us to these sanctuaries to find security and strength. Bless us, oh, Lord, that as we continue to hold fast to Your faith, we will eventually catch the wind of Your Spirit underneath our wings and soar high above whatever troubles are before us. We long to walk the walk every day, doing as Jesus would do. We pray for Your strength and grace, like that of an eagle, so that we may truly become what You created us to be. Amen.

Chapter 10: An Eagle's Prayer

May the Lord direct your hearts into God's love and
Christ's perseverance.

2 Thessalonians 3:5

———————◆•◆•◆———————

Like eagles, humans relish their homes. Depending on the circumstances, sometimes you upsize and sometimes you downsize. Whichever
the case, most people need a place to call home. You could say, in
pun-like manner, the store was my home away from home, since it was
all about home interiors. It was filled with beautiful things and wasn't
such a bad place to go to work every day.

Toward the end, however, it wasn't so peaceful. The beautiful vignettes
of furniture and accessories looked disheveled and bare. No new items
had been purchased so there wasn't anything exciting and fresh. To
add insult to injury, customers acted like vultures. They began to take
advantage of the situation and the economy, not caring how frail this
whole situation had made me. There was no positivity there. No hope.
No peace. It was the last place I wanted to be.

Every day I had to pray for strength to make it to the end. I prayed for
the constant reminders to go away. I prayed for new financial security
for my family. I prayed for the twelve hundred feathers that could help
me rise above the affliction I was facing.

Like me, do you feel relief isn't coming fast enough? Are you crying out for affirmation that your prayers are being heard? The psalmist David assures our prayers are heard.

> God has surely listened and has heard my prayer.
>
> Psalm 66:19

Prayer is the most powerful asset you can have in your spiritual life. We are told time and time again that it is a vital link to God, our Father. It immediately brings us into the presence of His Holy Spirit.

We, as believers in God, in our Father, and in Jesus His Son, and in the teachings of the Bible, have the special advantage of having the road map to live our lives in a way that brings comfort and happiness. We have His promise that if we embrace our faith and trust in Him, He will provide protection from the things of this world that are not of His. He gives us permission to be who we are, because we are all His children.

If the desires of your heart are to be free of negative emotions and self-destructive behaviors, so that you may be free to lift your eyes toward the glory of God and be filled with His grace, then begin by praying 2 Corinthians 5:17.

> Therefore if any man is in Christ, he is a new creature: the old things passed away behold, new things have come.

I wrote a poem many, many years ago that related to another tough time in my life and remembered it somewhere along the way. At night, along with the Lord's Prayer, I would lift it up, feeling that it had carried me through once before and could do so again.

I call it a poem, but really it is more like one of the psalms lifted up by David, when he cries out to the Lord for help defeating his enemies, asking if God hears his prayers, and pleading for God's comfort. It ends with the following:

Uncloak this thing, so I may know the truth,
and know my true enemy.

Then take that cloak and wrap my heart,
slowly rock and lull the pain away.

Hushed sobs, come and go, come and go,
come and go.

And in this vain attempt to get from here to there,
it is unfathomable how it ever came to be.

Whenever I got to the part about being swaddled in a cloak, I envisioned being wrapped in God's comforting arms.

Prayer

Dear God, as it says in Philippians 3, "One thing I do: Forgetting what is behind and straining toward what is ahead, I press on toward the goal to win the prize for which God has called me heavenward in Christ Jesus."

Comfort me in darkness and keep me focused on prayer so that I weep no more. Replace my fear, my lack of understanding, and my pain with Your Holy Spirit. Let me go forward, forgetting what is behind me, and press on toward the goal and prize that is You. In Jesus' name, we pray. Amen.

Chapter 11: The Eagle Transforms

> Consider it pure joy, my brothers, whenever you face
> trials of many kinds, because you know that the testing
> of your faith develops perseverance. Perseverance must
> finish its work so that you may be mature and complete,
> not lacking anything.

James 1:2–4

If you were to ask me to share with you a high point in my career, I would without hesitation take you back to 1994, when I sat across the lunch table from my boss, the president of Concord Brokerage Services in Rochester, New York. I had taken him to lunch to tell him that my (now ex-) husband had accepted a job in Virginia and that the moving trucks were coming in just two weeks. I explained that my husband and I decided that I would remain in Rochester for as long it took to help hire and train someone to take my place. Or that I was prepared to go to Troy, Michigan, which is where our parent company was, and help them transition my responsibilities in-house there, if that was necessary.

While I waited in those brief moments of silence for his response, I was already hearing his voice in my head saying, "Don't worry. None of that will be necessary. Just tell me when your last day is." Imagine my surprise and my absolute honor when he looked up at me and instead asked, "Can I have until the year 2000?"

Now, if you were to ask for a low point in my career, it would undoubtedly be the last and final days of closing my store in Williamsburg, Virginia. It gave a whole new meaning to the old adage about being kicked when you are down. At that point, all remaining inventory in my store was marked to well below its cost. And every sale in those final days was earmarked to cover all the expenses of closing the store. Not only was I watching my dream die, I was losing a significant investment that, in the end, would leave me truly penniless. And yet, each and every morning, I would have to get up and go into the store, where I would be confronted with one customer after another who would ask for yet another 10 to 15 percent off. Some were heartless enough to remark, "What's it matter to you? You are already closing."

One day, I caught a customer switching tags on an oversized mirror that normally retailed for $495. The liquidation price was two hundred dollars and she switched it with a twenty-five-dollar tag, thinking I would not notice. Another customer badgered me over the price of two chairs, repeatedly asking for a two-for-one deal. Firm that I could not do that, I pleaded with him to stop asking. To that, he accused me of not thinking him a Christian man.

What they could not fathom was that it did matter to me. It mattered to me very much, because of the numerous effects the store's closing was having on my family.

I felt exposed. I felt raw. I felt like I was literally being picked apart to die. It was only by the saving grace of God that I ever made it through.

Like humans, eagles too feel vulnerable. Overexposure to the weather, lack of food, other, more dominant eagles … But if strong and resourceful, an eagle can live up to forty years. In order for them to reach such an advanced age, they must go through a "midlife crisis" called the molting season. It can be a very painful process that comes with great depression. The depression comes from being defenseless and exposed for the 150 days it takes to complete. That is nearly five months. It is a time they are rendered defenseless, and some eagles do not survive.

To fully embrace the pain of the molting process, imagine yourself an eagle. Make your way to a rock. Perch yourself upon it, and with your own beak, begin to pluck out your worn and matted feathers from your body. Once your feathers are gone, make your way to the nearest river or stream and wash away any remaining dirt and grime. Then again, fully exposed to all the elements, make your way back to your rock and climb back up to bask in the sun and heal. While waiting for your new feathers to emerge, rub your talons on the rock to sharpen and strengthen them, because they have become dull and ineffective for hunting. And once that is done, scrape your beak against the rock to remove the build-up of calcium that has also hindered your ability to hunt.

If you make it through your molting season, you will truly be touched by God's grace. As a transformed eagle, you will be able to hunt more effectively than before, you will have more vitality, and you will soar with greater grandeur. You will emerge truly healed, new, and transformed.

The high point of my career was that of a young eagle soaring high, resilient, and respected. The low point in my career was like a molting eagle. The hurt and pain seemed unbearable, and though logic told me others could empathize, it felt like no one could.

Now that I have emerged, I lack the words to explain what it all means. But I did find the following from *The Molting Eagle* by Peter Laue:

> Do not try to fix what cannot be fixed. Do not try to fix what should not be fixed. Endure the molting. Do not complain. Do not find fault with one another. Do not find fault with your leaders, educators, pastors, or priests. Bury your prejudices and your arrogance. Do not find fault with God. Do not find fault period. Trust and obey God and allow Him to strip away the calcified and self-centered part of your soul. Repent for lording it over others. Repent for wasting your strength and youth on trivial and selfish pursuits. Do not think of yourself more highly than you ought to. Do not peck another molting eagle to death.

It is by the sheer grace of God I made it through my molting process, and when you do too, remember this:

For it is by grace you have been saved, through faith—
and this not from yourselves, it is the gift of God.

Ephesians 2:8

Prayer

Dear God, Your saving grace is magnificent and we are grateful forever. As it is in 2 Corinthians 3:4, "Praise be to the God and Father of our Lord Jesus Christ, the Father of compassion and the God of all comfort, who comforts us in all our trouble." We have been rescued and You have delivered us in our hour of need, during these difficult times. Remain with us always, so as we transform, we may offer such comfort and grace to others.

Amen.

Chapter 12: The Eagle's Cry

Those who hope in the Lord will renew their strength.
They will soar on wings like eagles; they will run and
not grow weary, they will walk and not be faint.

Isaiah 4:31

In the last chapter, I talked about the pain and suffering of the molting season. What I saved for this chapter is that during its season, you can often hear a molting eagle's billowing cry from afar. Likewise, when an eagle gets sick, it will fly to a nearby valley to recover or die, and often one can hear its distant echoes as well—its crying out.

Those are facts that make my heart ache. I have come to know this majestic bird as being strong and resilient. It hadn't occurred to me that it might need to take refuge and cry. In fact, somewhere on the outskirts of Phoenix there is a place called The Valley of the Crying Eagle. The mere thought that there is such a place hurts my heart.

I am consoled, however, knowing that when eagles fly to such sanctuaries, they are not alone. Although the eagle is known to be a bird of prey, it is also considered to be a bird of great compassion.

When we hear the word *compassion*, our natural tendency is to connect to its meaning in human form. But not all acts of compassion are reserved for humans. An eagle's act of compassion comes when strong and healthy eagles fly into the valleys where ailing eagles go, bringing food to the sick and offering encouragement to try to get the weak to fly again. It is this act of reaching out in times of distress which demonstrates their ability to act compassionately. It is irrefutably done with heart, given that healthy eagles do not stay in the valley yet return again and again to continue to help and offer compassion.

Here, I will be bold enough to liken my Job Transition Group to a sanctuary for crying eagles. It was my haven when I was in distress. It allowed me to cry out. It nurtured me. It offered compassion time and time again and provided the eagle-like, positive influences that helped me transform.

I've shared with you one of the high points in my career, which I likened to a young eagle soaring high. I earned the respect of my mentor. I was able to provide for myself. I was capable of facing storms head on and without fear. I also shared a low point in my career, when I felt like I was being picked apart to die like a molting eagle. I was vulnerable and afraid, and I thought I would not survive.

If you will recall, the molting process takes 150 days or nearly five months to complete. My molting process began the day we decided to close the store and continued for nearly eight months after we shut the doors for good. In total, eleven months. Members of this group back then can attest to how it rendered me defenseless, in pain, and depressed. I had no feathers to mount up and fly. I had no feathers to help carry me to safety. I was completely exposed to all the elements, and my transition group heard my cries.

Contrary to the quote I shared last chapter from Peter Laue, I did not endure my molting season well. I tried to fix that which did not need fixing. I complained. Although I tried hard not to find fault with my family and friends, I did. I found fault with leaders and mentors who I felt let me down. I especially found fault with customers whom I felt pecked me to death during my already painful molting season.

But the one thing I remained vigilant in was not finding fault with God. I trusted Him and I stayed focused, knowing that through Him, all things are possible. I prayed hard for Him to strip away the calcified and self-centered part of my soul. And in His time, He indeed did.

The Job Transition Group was also my rock—the rock upon which I was perched—where I began my healing, my renewal, and my transformation. Each time I cried out, another member came forward with compassion and gave me encouragement to fly again. Through God's saving grace, and the compassion of my support group's members, my new feathers emerged and I took flight.

I am a witness to all that manifests through my group. I began my journey facing a storm that I could not mount up against. And in the face of spiritual death, God gave me a haven to heal and a family of like-minded eagles to commune with. Through His teachings, I reclaimed my faith, my self-awareness, my determination, and my discipline. I regained my confidence, my resiliency, and my respect—all eagle-like characteristics.

In July of 2010, my transformation came full circle when the Job Transition Group asked me to be its leader. Now I have the blessings and opportunities each week to reach out to others in distress and offer my heart and my compassion.

The eagle goes through so many transformations to be the majestic, courageous, and inspirational creature we love. From the first time, it spreads its wings and catches the wind to emerging victoriously from its molting season. I am a transformed eagle, and who I am today is proof that there is truth in God's words and the lessons of the Scriptures.

> Blessed is the man who perseveres under trial, because
> when he has stood the test, he will receive the crown of
> life that God has promised to those who love him.

James 1:12 NIV

Those who hope in the Lord will renew their strength. They will soar on wings like eagles; they will run and not grow weary, they will walk and not be faint.

Isaiah 40:31

The third time he said to him, "Simon son of John, do you love me?" Peter was hurt because Jesus asked him the third time, "Do you love me?" He said, "Lord, you know all things; you know that I love you." Jesus said, "Feed my sheep."

John 21:17

Amen.

Exercise 1: Taking Flight Checklist

Your journey to spiritual enlightenment during job transition began twelve chapters ago with charts we called Your Preflight Checklist. The discomfort and inadequacies you may have felt before your journey should now feel less overwhelming. You should feel stronger and renewed now that you understand the right from wrong, truth from falsehood, and good and evil beliefs that kept you grounded. (See chapter 1.)

Take a moment to reevaluate your emotions and compare your progress to your preflight scores. In chart 1, your scores should have shifted from right to left. And in chart 2, they should have shifted from left to right.

With your new self-confidence and eagerness to learn and continue growing, brave asking a friend or family his or her opinion of your scores to truly see if you are being as honest as possible.

Chart 1 ⟵────────────────────

Date:	Somewhat							Overwhelming		
	1	2	3	4	5	6	7	8	9	10
Raw										
Exposed										
Picked Apart										
Deflective										
Negative										
Depressed										
Defenseless										
Lack of Desire										

Chart 2

Date:	Less Strong							More Strong		
	1	2	3	4	5	6	7	8	9	10
Self-Aware										
Determined										
Disciplined										
Confident										
Faithful										
Resilient										
Respected										
Compassionate										

Exercise 2: Look toward the Future by Learning from the Past

Throughout your search, people will ask

o Who are you?

o What do you do?

o What do you want to do?

You have to be able to answer these confidently and directly. Fear, however, can make you defensive, distant, and demanding. When you fear your weakness, or people point it out, you may retaliate and unknowingly act defensively. Although you will want to respond and act openly and honestly, you may inadvertently send mixed messages. In your attempt to say just the right thing, you may not come across as genuine. Worse yet, you may come across as unapproachable or standoffish. The more insecure you are, the more you may try to control or dominate things. Overtalking or feeling the need to have the last word is always a symptom of fear and insecurity.

Overcoming your fears is a stepping-stone to your success. But success doesn't simply start on the first day of your new job! It begins with how you prepare for the interview. Making a list of your past work experience, your skill sets, and your previous successes helps you prepare your résumé and cover letters. Doing this also helps you prepare for both telephone and in-person interviews.

Just as important as the lists of experience, skill sets, and achievements is a list of negative and positive emotions associated with job transition. As we have explored throughout this book, the healing process includes self-awareness of your emotions and your actions. Emotions and actions, like the heart and the mind—see chapter 5—are codependent in how we come across to others.

In his book *Survivor Personality,* Al Siebert explains "why some people are stronger, smarter, and more skillful at handling life's difficulties." Below are three adapted exercises that will help get you started. Do them as often as necessary until you feel you have truly shifted your thinking away from negative thoughts and remain more focused on the positive.

1) **Get it out.** Studies show that journaling or writing things down helps to put your emotions in check. Spending the time to get it all out will help you get rid of fear, anger, and damaging body language that may surface during an interview. Starting with the negative circumstances, expressing your feelings and emotions will be cathartic.

Exercise: Write down something you wish you had said to a former boss.

2) **Positive perspective.** Once emptied of the negativity, you can begin to focus on the positive. Recollecting positive experiences from the past will help rewrite the feelings of insecurity and uncertainty and help you gain perspective. By building your list of positive experiences, you will be building your self-esteem.

Exercise: Write down one thing or one activity from a previous job that you enjoyed doing.

3) **Think of the unexpected.** Now on the track to having your emotions in check, it is important to begin seeking out new opportunities. As discussed, having eagle eyes is seeing the big picture, and this exercise will help you see beyond the moment. Begin by thinking of a time when the outcome was more positive than what you had expected. Recall how you may have been discouraged at first but got encouraged once you were able to see a new possibility.

Exercise: Write down a time from any time in your career that had a more positive outcome than expected.

Exercise 3: Eagle Eye Job Search

The easiest way to connect with our greater good is to disconnect from all that is not. Making your way to the other side of job transition is no different. It requires disconnecting yourself from the things prohibiting you from reaching your goals. It doesn't matter if you are searching for a job or an entrepreneur searching for direction and momentum, the principle is the same. Pare down and make it simple. My dear friend, Reverend Alicia Leslie, says, "Let go of the many toys that confuse and make you cranky, in order to find the one you want to play with."

Take a look at the past week.

o   Where did you go?

o   What did you do?

o   How did you do it, and why?

o   Who did you spend time with?

o   Was it meaningful or empty?

o   Did it move you toward what matters most in your life?

o   How much time, energy, and money did you invest in these things?

o   Did those actions bear any fruit?

For those of you who need a bit more help on how to scale things back in order be more productive in your job search or job quest, try this method of organization that is based on the premise that each day presents a new beginning. No fall-out from the day before!

Monday morning—Make any follow-up calls necessary from the week before. Search for job opportunities in the morning. (Find at least two.)

Monday afternoon—Use the afternoon to tailor your résumé and cover letter to fit these two new prospects. *Do not send them out!*

Tuesday morning—Review and make changes to your résumé and cover letter in the morning. There will inevitably need to be minor tweaks.

Tuesday afternoon—Send them out in the afternoon, no later than 4:00 p.m.

Wednesday morning—This is a working day, a networking day, so go hang out with other eagles. Go to a networking event or have a meeting with someone who can help you assimilate eagle-like qualities or make connections for job prospects.

Wednesday afternoon—Take Wednesday afternoon "off." Reflect on what happened in your morning meetings. Run errands. Taking the time to take care of yourself midweek will support the energy and sense of accomplishment from networking.

Thursday morning—Refresh your memory of what transpired on Wednesday by making a list of recommendations or ideas discussed. Begin finding two more jobs to apply for.

Thursday afternoon—Tailor résumés and covers letter accordingly. *Do not send them out.*

Friday morning—Review résumés and cover letters for minor revisions.

Friday afternoon—Send them out.

With this schedule in good rotation, every Monday morning you'll have four jobs to make follow-up calls on and you'll have more than the minimum number of contacts to qualify for unemployment payments.

It will help you keep your momentum and provide for a good mix of searching, networking, and following-up. You'll even have time to take care of some things you can't do on the weekends.

Spend time in the evenings with family and friends in prayer and relaxation. This can help greatly with decision making, as we distance ourselves from "the world," and become, as Jesus said, "in the world, but not of it."

Job transition can so easily consume us, and alongside that, we have to deal with money, health, family, and recreation. Just remember to pare down and keep it simple. You can do it, as long as you do it from a foundation of what matters most. Become a master of your thoughts and feelings, using the Holy Spirit as your guide.

Exercise 4: Flying with Other Eagles

Letters of recommendation are an integral part of looking for employment. Most people are familiar with their nature. Notes of accomplishments, on the other hand, are not as familiar. Simply put, they can get you thinking more positively quicker. To help distinguish between the two, let's first look at each definition:

rec·om·men·da·tion:

1. The act of recommending.

2. Something that recommends, especially a favorable statement concerning character or qualifications.

3. Something, such as a course of action, that is recommended.

ac·com·plish·ment:

1. Something that has been achieved successfully.

2. The successful achievement of a task.

This quick comparison demonstrates that a recommendation is a statement or action holding value or merit, and an accomplishment is an achievement or success. Notes of accomplishments can serve to remind us of our value without going through the formality of securing a formal letter of recommendation. They are shorter, fast, and easy to get someone to respond to, and they will, without question, lift your mood, your attitude, and your self-esteem.

Notes of accomplishment are one or two quick paragraphs and speak to a job well done, a time when you went above and beyond on a project, or when you made a positive change in your behavior. They are structured in a way to help you learn how to approach someone to ask for his or her input. Prepare ahead of time by filling in the blanks. Practice what it says, and when comfortable, ask the person whose name appears in the first blank by reiterating what it says.

The examples below speak to a different type of need or accomplishment.

Highlights from Time Spent Together

Person to Contact: _____

Spent time together doing: _____

I really appreciate the extra time you've been spending with me on _____ .

It's people like you who make this transition easier. I was wondering if you would consider writing a quick note (one or two paragraphs) that highlights something positive from our time together. These words of encouragement will help me stay focused in working toward my next goal.

Words of Encouragement

Person to Contact: _____

Things you have discussed: _____

Your positive attitude has had a tremendous influence on me in achieving my goals. As I strive to meet my next objective of _____ _____, I would truly appreciate your support with a few words of encouragement that I can carry around with me for the times I need a little reminder of all I have accomplished.

Positive Changes

Person to Contact: _____

Project you worked on together: _____

I feel very lucky to have someone with your experience to guide me through some of the challenges I am facing. I really appreciate the time you have spent with me on _____ _____ _____. Your insights and advice have been invaluable.

As I move forward on implementing your suggestions, I was wondering if you could write down a few reminders of the positive changes you have seen in our work together.

Exercise 5: Eagle Instincts

The Job Transition Group (JTG) is often asked, "Why on Wednesdays?" and "Why at 7 a.m.?" Yes, 7 a.m. is certainly bright and early. And members often admit it is tough to get to the morning meetings, especially in the winter months when it is still dark and often chilly. As a coffee aficionado, getting a cold car is no fun before the first cup of coffee! But it is nice knowing there is fresh coffee waiting for all those who come.

Throughout the years, the group has considered different days and times, but the answer has remained the same.

Wednesday is the perfect day because it is over-the-hump day! It is the perfect day to receive an emotional adjustment, or perhaps an attitude adjustment, from the stress and challenges encountered on Monday and Tuesday. It refocuses us on what matters and provides the thrust to go about it as God wants us to.

For me, 7 a.m. is perfect, because the wonderful camaraderie and inspirational messages wrap us in God's embrace.

I cannot imagine a better way to start a day.

With Monday and Tuesday starting the workweek, Wednesday is seen as the day of the week to get past to start heading toward our beloved weekends. Research demonstrates a direct correlation between the days of the week and our moods.

Sunday	Monday	Tuesday	Wednesday	Thursday	Friday	Saturday

Most people have "down" moods on Mondays. Most people have "up" moods on Fridays. That holds true for you and those you will encounter in your job search. Begin monitoring your own moods throughout the week. Pay particular attention to how your mood changes with the various activities you engage in. Once you become more aware of how you are responding to your environment, people, and your activities, the more effective you will become.

Here are a couple of ideas to consider when managing your workweek based upon your mood:

o   Engage in an uplifting activity midweek that will reset your attitude, your outlook, and your mood. That could mean a group like my JTG. It could be a business networking group or even coffee with a follow eagle or two. You can form your own group of eagles. They will help you stay focused and energized.

o   When possible, avoid scheduling interviews on Mondays. If you have a choice to choose another day of the work, do so. This will keep you in better spirits on the weekend, knowing you will have time on Monday to prepare. And you can work in follow-up calls and notes immediately afterward, when your mood should already be positive as you approach the later part of the week.

Implementing strategies such as these will further your efforts to be more self-aware. Adapting this routine will nourish you midweek and fill your positivity bank. Over time, making better choices will become instinctual.

Trust in the Power of God's Word

The following is a note from someone unable to come to the Job Transition Group anymore because the person found a job. Thank God! I want to share this note with you, so you can trust in the power of the Holy Spirit and all God has in store for you. You will be lifted in His glory and purpose.

> When we talked last time, I told you how important the Job Transition Group had been for me, in giving me a biblical perspective on my situation. It helped me to hang on to what God had in store for me instead of rushing off in a panic to take the first job I could get. If I had done that, I would never have found myself in this current position, which has tangible and intangible benefits I would never have even imagined.
>
> One thing I should have said is how important every single individual is to the group and how every one of them has made an impact on me. I know that God placed me there to ease me through the emotional trials, providing relief and peace.

Scripture References

Introduction

2 Corinthians 1:3–4
Praise be to the God and Father of our Lord Jesus Christ, the Father of compassion and the God of all comfort, who comforts us in all our troubles, so that we can comfort those in any trouble with the comfort we ourselves receive from God.

Chapter 1

James 1:12
Blessed is the man who perseveres under trial, because when he has stood the test, he will receive the crown of life that God has promised to those who love him.

Jeremiah 29:10–12
For I know the plans I have for you," declares the Lord, plans to prosper you and not to harm you, plans to give you hope and a future.

Jeremiah 31:16
Restrain your voice from weeping and your eyes from tears, your work will be rewarded.

Chapter 2

2 Corinthians 4:17–18
For our light and momentary troubles are achieving for us an eternal glory that far outweighs them all. So we fix our eyes not on what is seen, but on what is unseen, since what is seen is temporary, but what is unseen is eternal.

Chapter 3

Psalm 71:20–21
Though you have made me see troubles, many and bitter, you will restore my life again; from the depths of the earth you will again bring me up. You will increase my honor and comfort me once more.

Isaiah 40:31
Those who hope in the Lord will renew their strength. They will soar on wings like eagles …

Psalm 139:7–10
Where can I go from Your Spirit? Or where can I flee from your presence? If I ascend into heaven, you are there; If I make my bed in hell, behold, you are there. If I take the wings of the morning, and dwell in the uttermost parts of the sea, even there your hand shall lead me, and your right hand shall hold me.

Isaiah 40:31
But those who hope in the Lord will renew their strength. They will soar on wings like eagles; they will run and not grow weary, they will walk and not be faint.

Chapter 4

Philippians 4:8
Finally, brothers and sisters, whatever is true, whatever is noble, whatever is right, whatever is pure, whatever is lovely, whatever is admirable—if anything is excellent or praiseworthy—think about such things.

Jeremiah 49:22
Look! An eagle will soar and swoop down, spreading its wings …

Chapter 5

Mark 8:18
Do you have eyes but fail to see, and ears but fail to hear? And don't you remember …?

Psalm 121:1–2
I lift up my eyes to the mountains—where does my help come from? My help comes from the Lord, the Maker of heaven and earth.

Chapter 6

John 14:18
I will not leave you as orphans; I will come to you.

Proverbs 3:8
This will bring health to your body and nourishment to your bones.

Proverbs 3:7–8
Do not be wise in your own eyes; fear the Lord and shun evil. This will bring health to your body and nourishment to your bones.

Chapter 7

Psalm 103:4:5
Who redeems your life from the pit and crowns you with love and compassion, who satisfies your desires with good things so that your youth is renewed like the eagle's.

Psalm 106:6
The Lord works righteousness and justice for all the oppressed.

Philippians 4:6–7
Do not be anxious about anything, but in every situation, by prayer and petition, with thanksgiving, present your requests to God. And the peace of God, which transcends all understanding, will guard your hearts and your minds in Christ Jesus.

Psalm 20 1:9
May the Lord answer you when you are in distress;   may the name of the God of Jacob protect you. May he send you help from the sanctuary and grant you support from Zion. May he remember all your sacrifices and accept your burnt offerings. Selah May he give you the desire of your heart and make all your plans succeed. We will shout for joy when you are victorious and will lift up our banners in the name of our God.

May the LORD grant all your requests. Now I know that the LORD saves his anointed; he answers him from his holy heaven with the saving power of his right hand. Some trust in chariots and some in horses, but we trust in the name of the LORD our God. They are brought to their knees and fall, but we rise up and stand firm. O LORD, save the king!

Amos 3:7
For the Lord God does nothing without revealing his secret to his servants the prophets.

Chapter 8

Philippians 3:13–14
One thing I do: Forgetting what is behind and straining toward what is ahead, I press on toward the goal to win the prize for which God has called me heavenward in Christ Jesus.

Psalm 51:10
Create in me a pure heart, O God, and renew a steadfast spirit within me.

Isaiah 41:9–11
So do not fear, for I am with you; do not be dismayed, for I am your God. I will strengthen you and help you; I will uphold you with my righteous right hand.

Philippians 4:12–14
I can do all this through him who gives me strength.

Exodus 15:1–3
The LORD is my strength and my defense; he has become my salvation. He is my God, and I will praise him, my father's God, and I will exalt him.

2 Samuel 22:32–34
It is God who arms me with strength and keeps my way secure.

1 Timothy 4:5–7
If you point these things out to the brothers and sisters, you will be a good minister of Christ Jesus, nourished on the truths of the faith and of the good teaching that you have followed.

2 Corinthians 1:3–4
Praise be to the God and Father of our Lord Jesus Christ, the Father of compassion and the God of all comfort, who comforts us in all our troubles …

1 Thessalonians 5:11
Therefore encourage one another and build each other up, just as in fact you are doing.

Hebrews 3:13
But encourage one another daily, as long as it is called "Today," so that none of you may be hardened by sin's deceitfulness.

Hebrews 10:25
Not giving up meeting together, as some are in the habit of doing, but encouraging one another—and all the more as you see the Day approaching.

Matthew 7:9–11
Which of you, if your son asks for bread, will give him a stone? Or if he asks for a fish, will give him a snake? If you, then, though you are evil, know how to give good gifts to your children, how much more will your Father in heaven give good gifts to those who ask him!

Ephesians 4:32
Be kind and compassionate to one another, forgiving each other, just as in Christ God forgave you.

1 Thessalonians 5:22–24
May God himself, the God of peace, sanctify you through and through. May your whole spirit, soul and body be kept blameless at the coming of our Lord Jesus Christ.

2 Chronicles 16:9
For the eyes of the LORD range throughout the earth to strengthen those whose hearts are fully committed to him.

Chapter 9

Deuteronomy 33:27
The eternal God is your dwelling place, and underneath are the everlasting arms.

Chapter 10

2 Thessalonians 3:5
May the Lord direct your hearts into God's love and Christ's perseverance.

2 Corinthians 5:17
Therefore if any man is in Christ, he is a new creature: the old things passed away behold, new things have come.

Ephesians 2:8
For it is by grace you have been saved, through faith—and this not from yourselves, it is the gift of God.

Chapter 11

James 1:2–4
Consider it pure joy, my brothers, whenever you face trials of many kinds, because you know that the testing of your faith develops perseverance. Perseverance must finish its work so that you may be mature and complete, not lacking anything.

2 Corinthians 3–4
Praise be to the God and Father of our Lord Jesus Christ, the Father of compassion and the God of all comfort, who comforts us in all our trouble.

Chapter 12

Isaiah 40:31
Those who hope in the Lord will renew their strength. They will soar on wings like eagles; they will run and not grow weary, they will walk and not be faint.

James 1:12 NIV
Blessed is the man who perseveres under trial, because when he has stood the test, he will receive the crown of life that God has promised to those who love him.

John 21:17
The third time he said to him, "Simon son of John, do you love me?" Peter was hurt because Jesus asked him the third time, "Do you love me?" He said, "Lord, you know all things; you know that I love you." Jesus said, "Feed my sheep.

About the Author

Regina K. Leigh is an entrepreneur, business strategist, and advocate for the unemployed. She continually expands her business ventures, creating partnerships and collaborative efforts to support and transform people, businesses, and organizations into stronger, richer entities. Her own business-consulting firm, Leigh Management Consulting, assists businesses in securing the capital they need to grow. It also provides national corporate training for human capital analytics and workforce development.

It is Regina's calling to facilitate the Job Transition Group (JTG) in Williamsburg, Virginia. The JTG is an interdenominational, Christian-based ministry that provides emotional and spiritual support to help individuals overcome the challenges of losing a job as well as searching for and regaining employment. Established in 2003, Regina took the reigns as facilitator for the group in 2010. Each week, her thought-provoking devotionals and community outreach effects positive change. Scripture and occupational challenges come full circle as she teaches how to stay strong in faith and in a relationship with God while facing adversity and uncertainty.

Regina's passion to help others is rooted in the challenges she faced in finding her way again, after the dream that took her fifteen years to build was swiftly taken away as a result of the downturn of the economy. She freely shares the losses, setbacks, and successes of this experience with those she helps.

Regina shares a life blessed with love and laughter with her husband, who she fondly calls her "Handsome Thomas G." She feels privileged to have a loving and positive relationship with Tom's three children and their two grandchildren. Tom and Regina enjoy traveling, sailing, and exercising together. To honor their commitment to each other, every Friday night is "date night." No exceptions.

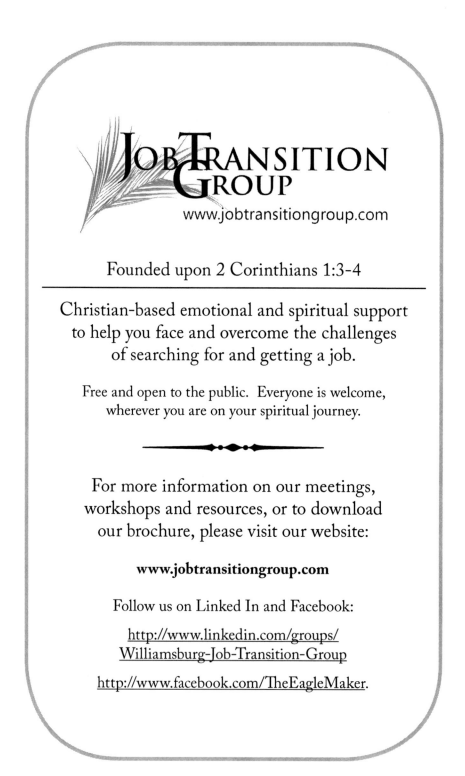

JobTransition Group

www.jobtransitiongroup.com

Founded upon 2 Corinthians 1:3-4

Christian-based emotional and spiritual support
to help you face and overcome the challenges
of searching for and getting a job.

Free and open to the public. Everyone is welcome,
wherever you are on your spiritual journey.

For more information on our meetings,
workshops and resources, or to download
our brochure, please visit our website:

www.jobtransitiongroup.com

Follow us on Linked In and Facebook:

http://www.linkedin.com/groups/
Williamsburg-Job-Transition-Group

http://www.facebook.com/TheEagleMaker.

Want to Target Your Job Search Efforts?

Learn and Understand Your
Performance Strengths

Overcome Your Stress and Fear

Get Hired Faster

Your JOURNEY Begins Here

Understanding your strengths and talents can help in
being more successful in finding employment!

Having an objective view of your performance factors is
the best asset for charting a pathway to success!

Knocking down emotional barriers and overcoming stress builds confidence!

The ProScan® is the most powerful tool you can use in your job
transition

The PDP ProScan® Identifies Your Performance Factors

- Cornerstone Performance Traits that help you identify the right role for you
- Energy styles and levels that fuel your performance
- Satisfaction levels associated with your goals and aspirations
- Current energy drains and stresses that are creating barriers

The PDP ProScan® is fast, accurate, and straightforward to help you implement a
plan for success

- Takes only minutes to complete
- Receive personalized results in easy to understand, well-organized, and
  comprehensive reports

Take Your ProScan today! Visit Leigh Management
Consulting at www.mybusinessforce.com

CPSIA information can be obtained at www.ICGtesting.com
Printed in the USA
BVOW031513071212

307312BV00001B/2/P